3e

e for English

A2 → B1

workbook

Coordination pédagogique
Mélanie Herment
Professeur, formatrice
Académie de Paris

Auteurs
Mathias Degoute
Professeur
Académie de Paris

Camille Dumas
Professeur
Auckland, Nouvelle-Zélande

Julien Herbreteau
Professeur
Académie de Versailles

Mélanie Herment

Karine Letellier
Professeur
Académie de Paris

Grammaire et prononciation
Denis Jamet
Professeur des Universités en Linguistique anglaise
Université Jean Moulin – Lyon 3

didier

Édition : Sandrine Paniel
Responsable d'édition : Catherine Laurent
Iconographie : María Mora
Conception graphique de la couverture : Marie-Astrid Bailly-Maître et Léo Pico
Adaptation de la maquette intérieure et mise en page : Catherine Sèvegrand
Illustrations : Sylvie Eder
Cartographie et infographie : Jean-Pierre Crivellari (pp. 73 ; 105-106) et Vincent Landrin (p. 114)
Documents : Isabelle Aubourg
Photogravure : RVB photogravure

Références iconographiques
couv (b)Bryan Reinhart/Masterfile ; (h) Green Light/Bettmann/Corbis ; (m) Warren Bolster/Stone/Gettyimages ; 4 (hd) : Ann Makosinski ; 4 (hg) : Eric Chen ; 5 : yaviki-Fotolia.com, opificio 42/Cultura/Corbis ; 13 : Ian West/PA Wire/Abacapress.com ; 19 (mg) : Elena Blokhina-Fotolia.com ; 22 (bg) : "8 Mile", Curtis Hanson with Eminem, 2002 © Imagine Entertainment/Collection ChristopheL ; 22 (m) : IMDb ; 23 : IMDb ; 26 : Celtx.com ; 60 : Alekss-Fotolia.com ; 68 (1) : Bateau rouge rue : Philippe Lopez/Afp ; rue : Toru Yamanaka/Afp ; 69 (2) : Voiture dans chemin de fer : Toru Yamanaka/Afp ; chemin de fer: Toshifumi Kitamura/Afp ; 69 (3) : Bateau sur maison : Yasuyoshi Chiba/Afp ; rue maison : Toshifumi Kitamura/Afp ; 69 (bg) : "The Day after tomorrow", Roland Emmerich, 2004 © 20 th Century Fow/Album/AKG ; 73 (h) : Copyright © 2014 Dictionary.com ; 76 : Journeyman Pictures ; 81 : New Zealand Post ; 88 : Geoatlas.com ; 100-103 : taitai6769-Fotolia.com ; 106 (bg) : US Department of Commerce, US Census ; 106 (hg) : To-Hawaii.com ; 123 (bmg) : "Ghost Rider", Mark Steven Johnson with Nicolas Cage © Columbia Pictures Corporation/Collection ChristopheL ; 123 (bg) : "Iron Man", Jon Favreau with Robert Downey Jr © Paramount Pictures, Marvel Enterprises/Collection ChristopheL ; 123 (bm) "Wonder Woman", William M. Marston with Linda Carter, 1975 © Bruce Lansbury Productions, Douglas S. Cramer Company, Warner Bros./Collection ChristopheL ; 123 (bmg) :"The Avengers", Joss Whedon with Chris Evans, 2012 © Marvel Enterprises/The Kobal Collection/Picture Desk ; 123 (bd) : "Thor: The Dark World", Alan Taylor with Christopher Yost © Marvel Studios/Collection ChristopheL ; 130 : "I got my yearbook today!" Ashley Siu, http://www.youtube.com/watch?v=EujZELu3OCk ; 132 (mc) : Maya Tairy/Agefotostock ; 132 (md) : Picture Patners/Alamy ; 132 (mg) : Jeff Greenberg 4 of 6/Alamy ; 134-139 : nous remercions très chaleureusement les établissements Highgate School (Londres) et Toms River High School North (New Jersey) pour leur précieuse contribution ; Drapeaux France et Angleterre : Geoatlas.com

Références textes
25, 35, 39, 42, 43 : "The Soul of Butterfly" by Muhammad Ali and Hana Yasmeen Ali, 2004, Bantam Press ; 44 : "How to Conduct an Interview" Copyright © Scholastic Inc./Scholastic Teachers. Used by permission. ; 46 : New York Media ; 57 : Tony Rogers/journalism.about.com ; 58 : Tom McCarthy, Matt Wells, Adam Gabbatt, Katie Rogers, Warien Murray/The Guardian 29/10/2012 ; 60 : Copyright © Joanne Harris. Reproduced by permission of the author c/o Rogers, Coleridge & White Ltd., 20 Powis Mews, London W111JN ; 75 : Rotorua Daily Post ; 77 : The New Zealand Herald ; 79 : TheFreeDictionary © 2012 by Farlex Inc. ; 90 : Paroles "Miss you" : Mick Jagger and Richard Keith, 1978 © Avec l'aimable autorisation de Emi Music Publishing France ; 95 : "Frank Ferdinand to allow fans to pick BBC Radio 6 Music Festival Setlis", Sam Rigby, 3/02/2014, Digital Spy ; 101 : Agatha Christie: "An Autobiography" Copyright © 1922 Agatha Christie Limited. All rights reserved. Agatha Christie, Poirot and Miss Marple are registered trade marks of Agatha Christie Limited in the UK and/or elsewhere. All rights reserved ; 102 : reprinted from the June 1993 issue of Condé Nast Traveler. Copyright © 1993 by Rick Bass. Reprinted by permission of the author ; 108 (2h) : Agatha Christie: "An Autobiography" Copyright © 1922 Agatha Christie Limited. All rights reserved. Agatha Christie, Poirot and Miss Marple are registered trade marks of Agatha Christie Limited in the UK and/or elsewhere. All rights reserved ; 108 (2m, b) : reprinted from the June 1993 issue of Condé Nast Traveler. Copyright © 1993 by Rick Bass. Reprinted by permission of the author ; 113 : From "The Fun They Had" published in "The Best of Isaac Asimov" by Isaac Asimov, copyright 1973 by Isaac Asimov. used by permission of Doubleday, a division of Random House, Inc. ; 116 : Dr Marc Rayman/spaceplace.nasa.gov ; 118, 119 : Reprinted by permission of United Agents on behalf of: The Literary Executors of The Estate of H.G. Wells

PAPIER À BASE DE FIBRES RECYCLÉES

éditions didier s'engagent pour l'environnement en réduisant l'empreinte carbone de leurs livres. Celle de cet exemplaire est de :
400 g éq. CO_2
Rendez-vous sur www.editionsdidier-durable.fr

 – ISBN : 978-2-278-07906-3
Achevé d'imprimer en Italie en avril 2014 par LEGO PRINT (Lavis)
Dépôt légal : 7906/01

Sommaire

1 You've got talent!

Discover

The winners have been announced!

→ Textbook p. 12

2 a. Imagine you are one of the judges. Underline the elements you find particularly interesting in these two profiles, then explain your reasons.

Eric Chen, USA
Age: 17
Grade: Junior
Project: **a new anti-flu[1] medicine**

Passions: "Besides my love for math and science, clubs, volunteering and research, I enjoy playing the piano and fencing[2]."

Google Science Fair Project: "My project is to discover [...] a new type of anti-flu medicine, effective against all influenza viruses."

Why participate? "I feel like Google would be one of the biggest platforms for me to communicate my ideas to the world."

Ann Makosinski, Canada
Age: 15
Grade: Freshman
Project: **a battery-free flashlight**

Passions: "I have a great love for science [...]. I also have a great passion for insects, and I have a cat."

Google Science Fair Project: "My objective in my project was to create a flashlight that runs solely on the heat of the human hand."

Why participate? "I would feel much more motivated in my studies and career choices, knowing that someone believes in what I'm doing."

1. flu=influenza *(grippe)* **2.** *Escrime*

Comment on what you have underlined: . . . .

. . . .

. . . .

. . . .

. . . .

4 Your turn! Who won the last Google Grand Prize? Look it up on the internet and take notes in the grid below.

Google Grand Prize Winner in ....year........

Name of the winner: ....

Country of origin: .... Age: ....

Grade: ....

Name of the project: ....

Passions: ....

Short description of the project: ....

Why participate? ....

....

....

"14 – and already a pro!"

→ Textbook p. 13

Cooking prodigy Flynn McGarry

Place of residence: San Fernando Valley, USA.

Talent: At 14, he has already worked as the head chef at a fancy Beverly Hills restaurant.

When did he start? He started cooking for his family at 11.

Why did he start? "My mom didn't really like cooking, and when she did cook I didn't really like her food. And I was watching something on the Food Network, and I thought, 'I could do this'".

What next? "My goal? Three Michelin stars. Restaurant on the top 50 list, hopefully in the top five" McGarry says.

His advice? "Focusing on your passion and hard work definitely pay off in the end."

2 a. **Underline the words and expressions related to cooking.**

b. **Work on words. Insert the words you have underlined into the spidergram below, then think of more words related to cooking.**

Cooking

Places:

....
....
....
....

Jobs:

....
....
....
....

Media:

....
....
....

c. **What do you know or what can you imagine about:**

- the Food Network? ....
- three Michelin stars? ....

3 Need help? **Fill in this document about Quinn Sullivan.**

Talent: ....

Grade: ....

When did he start? ....

Why did he start? ....

....

How did he learn his talent? ....

....

What were the next steps?

At 6: ....

At 7: ....

This year: ....

More information: ....

....

....

Training Task

→ Textbook p. 13

What's your talent?

Take notes:

Bring a photo or an illustration related to your talent!

Your talent: ....

When did you start? ....

Why did you start? ....

....

Where do you practise? ☐ at home ☐ at school ☐ in a club

☐ other place: ....

What have you already achieved? ....

....

What would you like to do next?

- Meet .... • Take part in ....
- Work ....
- Other: ....

Understand

"The world's most wanted hacker"

→ Textbook p. 15

3 Need help? **The following elements describe key stages in Kevin Mitnick's life.**

a. Number them in chronological order.

☐ *serving time in prison* ☐ *hacking into friends' telephone systems (phone freaking)*

☐ *playing cat-and-mouse games with the government* ☐ *working as a consultant*

☐ *hacking into big companies' security systems*

b. **Use them to recap Kevin Mitnick's career.**

Training Task

→ Textbook p. 15

Help a teen choose a career

- **Read this letter and underline: in blue Melissa's experiences**
  in red what she enjoys doing.
- **Write down your reply, including some advice:**

From melissaroberts@gmail.com
Subject Help needed!
To careeradvisor@dreamjob.com

Reply | Forward | Junk | Delete

Dear career advisor,

My father was a Marine, so while growing up I've had the opportunity to live in many different places around the world, my favorites being Japan and Norway. I like to keep myself busy. My passion is music. I also enjoy acting and have performed in many different community theatre productions. Furthermore, in my free time I enjoy eating, hanging out with friends, watching movies, and hiking. What career could I choose?

Thank you for your help!

Melissa.

Words

1 *Words to remember* Vérifie que tu connais le vocabulaire du chapitre. → Textbook p. 17

LIVING YOUR PASSION

Interests

Écris la préposition manquante.

① be . . . . (music)

② be interested . . . . (computers)

③ have a great love/passion . . . . (science)

④ be highly passionate . . . . (teaching)

⑤ be a great fan . . . . (gymnastics)

Achievements

Comment dit-on en anglais...?

⑥ *recevoir un prix* = ...

⑦ *réussir à faire quelque chose* = (1) . . . .

(2) . . . .

⑧ *participer à* = ...

Practice

Retrouve les lettres manquantes.

⑨ tr _ _ n

⑩ ex _ _ _ _ _ _ e

⑪ re _ _ _ _ se

Personality

Donne un synonyme ou un antonyme.

⑫ lazy ≠ . . . .

⑬ stupid ≠ . . . . ,

. . . .

⑭ talented = ...

⑮ incredible = ...

⑯ imaginative = ...

⑰ precocious = ...

Personality

Retouve p. 17 de ton manuel des expressions pour caractériser le travail de ces personnages.

⑱ .... ≠ ⑲ ....

⑳ .... ㉑ ....

㉒ ....

2 **Relis le texte sur Flynn McGarry. Utilise les *Words to remember* p. 17 de ton manuel pour parler de ses centres d'intérêt, sa personnalité, son parcours… Enregistre-toi et ré-écoute ta performance.**

3 **Récapitulons ! Fais la liste de toutes les expressions utiles pour parler des sujets suivants.**

Interests/passions	Beginnings	Experiences and achievements	Projects
I'm into…	How did you get into hacking?	I got to meet Eric Clapton.	Where do I see myself ten years from now?

Grammar

Parcours de RÉVISIONS : LE PRÉSENT SIMPLE

a. Lis ces énoncés au Présent simple et complète le tableau.

Dans quels types de phrases l'auxiliaire est-il présent? ....

	Type de phrase : affirmative? négative? interrogative?
A. *I **enjoy** playing the piano and fencing.*	
B. *Where **do** I **see** myself ten years from now?*	
C. *My brother **doesn't share** my passion.*	
D. *He **prefers** cooking.*	

b. Les phrases C. et D. sont à la 3e personne du singulier.

Que doit-on alors ajouter à l'auxiliaire ou au verbe? ....

DÉDUIS !

Au Présent simple, l'auxiliaire .... ou .... (à la troisième personne du singulier) est très souvent nécessaire à la construction des phrases ☐ affirmatives ☐ négatives ☐ interrogatives.

La forme affirmative se construit généralement avec la base verbale du verbe ou cette base verbale + ... à la troisième personne du singulier.

1 Écris si tu pratiques ou non ces activités. Tu peux donner des détails :

1. Play chess.

....

2. Practise a sport.

....

3. Cook at home.

. . . .

4. Play an instrument.

. . . .

2 Voici ce qu'ont dit des célébrités au sujet de leur passion. Réécris ces textes, à la troisième personne du singulier, pour le magazine de ton école :

1. *Michael Jordan:* "I don't do things half-heartedly. Because I know if I do, then I can expect half-hearted results."

Michael Jordan . . . .

. . . .

2. *Sasha Azevedo:* "I run because it's my passion, and not just a sport."

Sasha Azevedo . . . .

. . . .

3. *Rihanna:* "I don't do things for the response or for the controversy. I just live my life."

Rihanna . . . .

. . . .

Parcours de RÉVISIONS : LE PRÉTÉRIT SIMPLE

a. Lis ces énoncés au Prétérit simple et complète le tableau.

Dans quels types de phrases l'auxiliaire est-il présent ? . . . .

	Type de phrase : affirmative ? négative ? interrogative ?
A. *My mom didn't really like cooking.*	
B. *How did you teach yourself the guitar?*	
C. *His parents gave him his first toy guitar when he was 3.*	
D. *That night, Guy called Quinn on stage to play.*	

b. Qu'observe-tu ?

– Dans les phrases ...., c'est l'auxiliaire qui porte la marque du Prétérit.

– Dans les phrases ...., c'est le verbe qui porte la marque du Prétérit.

c. Les énoncés C et D sont à la forme affirmative. Donne l'infinitif de :

gave: .... ⎤
was: .... ⎦ → Ce sont des verbes ....

called: .... → C'est un verbe ....
Formation : base verbale + ...

DÉDUIS !

On utilise le Prétérit pour raconter un événement ....

- **Forme négative :** sujet + auxiliaire .... + ... + ...
(négation)
- **Forme interrogative :** auxiliaire .... + sujet + ...
- **Forme affirmative :**
  1. verbe régulier : sujet + [base verbale + ...]
  2. verbe irrégulier : sujet + forme irrégulière (voir liste p. 173 de ton manuel)

3 Écris la biographie de Harry Styles selon les indications suivantes :

Birth: England, 1994
Family: Des Styles, father - Anne Cox, mother (divorced, 2001)
Influences: Elvis Presley
First Band: White Eskimo (lead singer)
Audition: the X Factor (2010)
First Album: Up All Night (2012)

....

....

....

. . . .

. . . .

. . . .

. . . .

. . . .

. . . .

1. PRÉSENT *HAVE* + PARTICIPE PASSÉ

a. Lis les énoncés suivants puis complète le tableau :

A. *Flynn* ***started*** *cooking for his family [at 11].*

B. *[At 14], Flynn* ***has*** *already* ***worked*** *as the head chef at a fancy restaurant.*

N.B. Flynn a 14 ans à ce jour.

Phrases	Formes verbales en bleu	Formation	Nom de la conjugaison
A		base verbale + ...	
B		auxiliaire . . . . (temps : . . . .) + ...	

Attention à la formation du participe passé :

- verbes réguliers : base verbale + *ed* (identique au Prétérit) ;
- verbes irréguliers : voir la liste dans ton manuel, p. 173.

b. Observe maintenant les mots entre crochets :

– En **A**, ils renvoient à un moment ☐ passé ☐ présent.

On peut donc en déduire que l'énonciateur :

☐ raconte ce qui s'est passé, comme on raconte une histoire.

☐ met en avant la situation au moment présent.

– En **B**, ils renvoient à un moment ☐ passé ☐ présent.

On peut donc en déduire que l'énonciateur :

☐ raconte ce qui s'est passé, comme on raconte une histoire.

☐ met en avant la situation au moment présent.

DÉDUIS !

Le Présent *Have* + participe passé est composé de :

auxiliaire . . . . conjugué au . . . . + ... du verbe.

Avec cette forme, l'énonciateur ne s'intéresse pas à l'événement passé en lui-même.

Il s'intéresse à ce qu'il dit du sujet au moment . . . .

4 Remember Flynn McGarry and Quinn Sullivan?

→ Textbook p. 15

Since then:

- Flynn McGarry has apprenticed at some of the best restaurants in the USA.
- Quinn Sullivan has given concerts in Canada.

What else have they done? Search the Internet, and tell your classmates about it.

. . . .

. . . .

. . . .

. . . .

5 Dis ce que tu as déja fait – ou non.

e.g. *I have already… / I have never…*

1. Take part in a talent show.
2. Invent or build a machine, for example with Lego bricks.
3. Win a competition, or take part in a competition.
4. Sing in front of an audience, for example for your family at Christmas.
5. Run more than 2 kilometers without stopping.

1. . . . .

2. . . . .

3. ....

4. ....

5. ....

Parcours de RÉVISIONS : LES QUESTIONS ET LES MOTS INTERROGATIFS

a. Lis les énoncés et complète ci-dessous :

	Ces questions interrogent sur... (chose / date / lieu/ moyen / raison /personne) → Sers-toi des réponses !	Composition de la forme verbale
A. *When did you start playing the guitar?* In 2008.		
B. *Why did he start cooking?* Because his mum didn't.		
C. *What have they done?* They have created amazing inventions.		
D. *What is your favorite class?* History.		
E. *Whom do you most admire?* My grandfather.		
F. *Where did you first play with Buddy Guy?* At the Zeiterion Theater, in New Bedford.		
G. *How did you teach yourself the guitar?* By watching a lot of guitarists playing.		

b. Quelle est la fonction des mots interrogatifs dans les phrases H et I ci-dessous ?

☐ sujet ☐ complément

Ces questions se construisent comme des phrases ☐ interrogatives ☐ affirmatives.

H. *Who won the last Google Grand Prize?*

I. *What makes these two boys "prodigies"?*

DÉDUIS !

- L'ordre des mots dans une question est en général :

(mot interrogatif) + ... + sujet + ...

- Le mot interrogatif :
  - . . . . interroge sur une chose.
  - . . . . interroge sur une date.
  - . . . . interroge sur un lieu.
  - . . . . interroge sur une raison.
  - . . . . interroge sur une personne.
  - . . . . interroge sur le moyen.

ATTENTION

- *Be* jouant le rôle à la fois de verbe et d'auxiliaire, il se suffit à lui-même dans une expression ou une négation.
- Lorsqu'un mot interrogatif est ☐ sujet ☐ complément, la question se construit comme une phrase affirmative (donc sans auxiliaire pour un temps simple).

6 Lis chacune des phrases suivantes. Quelles questions poserais-tu pour interroger sur les mots en gras ?

	Questions correspondantes
1. I was born **in Michigan.**	
2. I started learning tennis **when I was 5.**	
3. I can speak **four** languages.	
4. Tom practises **with famous musicians.**	
5. I have sung in **Canada and Mexico.**	
5. **Flynn's mom** didn't like cooking.	
6. **Hacking** is against the law.	

2. LE CONSEIL : *SHOULD / COULD*

a. Observe l'énoncé en italique et décompose les formes verbales.

Auxiliaire modal . . . . + ... + ... du verbe
(négation)

If you don't like getting dirty you shouldn't work with animals. You could write books about them, you write so well!

Auxiliaire modal . . . . + ... du verbe

b. Dans les deux cas, l'énonciateur donne un conseil. Dans quel cas s'appuie-t-il sur les capacités du sujet pour formuler ce conseil ?

☐ *you shouldn't work* Traduction : . . . .

☐ *you could write* Traduction : . . . .

Relève ce qui t'a guidé(e) : . . . .

DÉDUIS !

- Pour formuler un conseil, on peut employer : Sujet + ... + base verbale.
- Si ce conseil s'appuie sur les capacités du sujet : Sujet + ... + base verbale.

7 Quels métiers ou domaines de travail conseiller ? Fais des suggestions logiques.

1. If you love Maths, ...

2. If you like meeting people, ...

3. If you like doing sports, ...

4. If you are crazy about foreign languages, ...

5. If you don't like travelling, ...

6. If you don't like being outdoors, ...

8 **Destination secrète ! Choisis un pays ou une région, et écris des conseils de voyage pour des visiteurs. Lis ces conseils à ton groupe qui devra deviner ta destination. Commence tes conseils par :**

1. Don't . . . .

2. You should . . . .

3. You could . . . .

4. Why don't you . . . .

5. Don't forget to . . . .

6. You shouldn't . . . .

7. You could try. . . . .

9 **Tu participes à la rédaction de ce guide. Tu as choisi l'image ci-dessous pour illustrer ce qu'il ne faut pas faire si l'on veut réussir sa fête. Relève tout ce qui pourrait être amélioré, puis rédige quelques conseils.**

Pronunciation

❶ L'intonation des phrases affirmatives et interrogatives track 6

a. Écoute les phrases suivantes en faisant attention à l'intonation puis répète-les.

1. I was fascinated with the telephone system.

2. Do you think hacking is some sort of terrorism?

3. Why did you start hacking?

4. What did you do that got you arrested?

5. You don't look like a dangerous guy.

6. Did you get into hacking for the girls?

b. Toutes ces phrases ont-elles la même intonation ? ☐ Oui ☐ Non

Classe-les selon le type d'intonation :

Intonation	**Intonation** ....
Phrases :	Phrases : ....

c. Trace la courbe intonative des phrases selon les exemples ci-dessous :

I am a famous dancer.
What do you do?

Are you a famous dancer?

1. Do you have a special talent?

2. Yes, I do have a special talent.

3. What is your special talent?

4. I am very good at physics, and I want to find a cure against diseases.

5. How are you going to succeed in doing that?

6. First, I will have to go to university and graduate in physics.

d. Quelle conclusion en tires-tu ?

Très souvent, les phrases .... et .... en *WH-* ont une intonation descendante en fin de phrase, tandis que les phrases .... commençant par un auxiliaire (*have, be, do* et les modaux) ont une intonation montante.

Toutefois, selon les types d'anglais (britannique, américain, australien, etc.) et en fonction que ce que l'énonciateur souhaite exprimer, il peut y avoir des exceptions.

2 La prononciation des mots interrogatifs en *WH-* track 7

a. Écoute les mots interrogatifs en regardant leur transcription phonétique :

– what /wɒt/ (GB) /wɑːt/ (US)
– which /wɪtʃ/
– who /huː/
– whom /huːm/
– when /wen/
– where /weə/ (GB) /weər/ (US)
– why /waɪ/
– how /haʊ/

b. Répète au moins une fois la prononciation de chacun de ces mots.

c. Lis maintenant ces phrases à voix haute en faisant attention aux prononciations des mots interrogatifs en *WH-*, et à l'intonation de la phrase :

1. **What** was the turning point in your career?
2. **When** did you become really famous?
3. **How** did you manage to become successful?
4. **Who** helped you to become who you are now?
5. **Which** job would you like to do in the future?
6. **Why** have you chosen to turn your passion into your job?
7. **Where** do you think you'll live in 10 years?
8. **Whom** did you want to thank?

d. Fais un dialogue avec un camarade en lui demandant s'il a un talent, lequel, comment il peut s'en servir, pour faire quoi, etc. Jouez ce dialogue à l'oral devant vos autres camarades, en faisant attention à l'intonation des phrases et à la prononciation des mots interrogatifs.

2 Legends on screen

Discover

Let's go to the movies!

→ Textbook p. 25

2 Label the different pieces of information:

cast and crew – poster – release date – average rating – plot – genre – title – tagline

4 In groups.
Start completing the IMDb page of the film you have chosen.

tip
Sers-toi des images et des phrases d'accroche pour imaginer l'intrigue.

IMDb | Find Movies, TV shows, Celebrities and more... | All
Movies, TV & Showtimes | Celebs, Events & Photos | News & Community | Watchlist (139)

Print out the poster and paste it here!

.... (   ) Top 5000

U 110 min ....

Your rating: ★★★★★★★★★★ -/10

Ratings: [   ] /10 from 130 548 users Metascore: 77/100
Reviews: 541 user | 202 critic | 38 from Metacritic.com

....
....
....
....
....

Director: ....

Stars: ....
....

+ Watchlist | Watch Trailer | Share...

6 After listening to people, complete the page above with further information about your film (use a different colour).

Then go to www.imdb.com and check the real page!

Training Task

→ Textbook p. 25

The Hollywood Guessing Game!

- **Think about what you will say to help the class guess the title of your movie. Note down important words here:**

tiP

- Prends le temps de faire ton choix : que pourrais-tu dire du film que tu as choisi ? Il est parfois plus facile de parler d'un film qu'on n'a pas aimé !
- Pour te préparer à prendre la parole, aide-toi de la page *How to speak in front of an audience* → Textbook p. 22.

Title of the movie	
How you felt when you left the cinema	*Key adjectives:* *Verbs:*
The plot	*Keywords:*
The cast and crew	Names *and jobs:*

Understand

Ali, the biopic

→ Textbook p. 26

1 Pick out 4 criteria from the categories below to make your decision about the Oscar:

Subject
- ☐ an interesting character / hero
- ☐ a rather light-hearted / entertaining film
- ☐ a film with a profound subject

Communication
- ☐ a catchy title
- ☐ an attractive poster

Cast and crew
- ☐ a well-known actor
- ☐ an unknown but charismatic actor
- ☐ an actor who looks like the hero
- ☐ an experienced director

Ali's autobiography

→ Textbook p. 26

"There was no such thing as a Black superhero"

One Halloween, a little Black girl was trick-or-treating around the neighborhood, dressed up in a superhero costume, but her face was painted white. When I asked her why, she said that her sister told her that there was no such thing as a Black superhero. She was right. When I turned on the television, everyone was always White. Superman was White, Santa Claus was White. They even made Tarzan, king of the jungle in Africa, a White man. I noticed that Miss America was always White, and the president living in the White House was White, too. Nothing good reflected our image.

At that early age, I could see that something was very wrong. I didn't understand it. I thought that my skin was beautiful, I was proud of the color of my complexion. But everything black was considered bad, and undesirable. Like black cats bring bad luck. Devils' food cake was the dark cake, and angel food cake was the white cake. These may have been subtle messages, but the effects were profound. Every day these messages shaped the images that I and other non-white children had of ourselves. I didn't know how, but I knew that I was going to help my people. Somehow, I was going to make a difference in the world. The more injustice that I saw, the stronger my feelings grew. It made me feel that I was here for a reason. [...]

I thought boxing would help me be that public Black role model who was missing while I was growing up. I thought my purpose was to be that hero who showed children that Black is beautiful. I thought my purpose was to be that champion who showed White people they couldn't treat Blacks like second class citizens. I learned that all of these accomplishments were important, but even more important, I gained a platform that allowed me to carry out my real mission, which has been to encourage all people to respect each other and to live in peace.

The Soul of a Butterfly, Muhammad Ali, Hana Yasmeen Ali, 2004

2 a. To prepare your shooting, you need a good understanding of the situation. Choose different colours to underline the following information :

- **who?** (characters, age, identity, costumes...)
- **when?** (in the narrator's life, but also what time of the year, what time of the day...)
- **where?**
- **what?** (actions, feelings...)

c. Here is a scriptwriting tool called CELTX, used by professionals to prepare their scripts. Look at how this script is written:

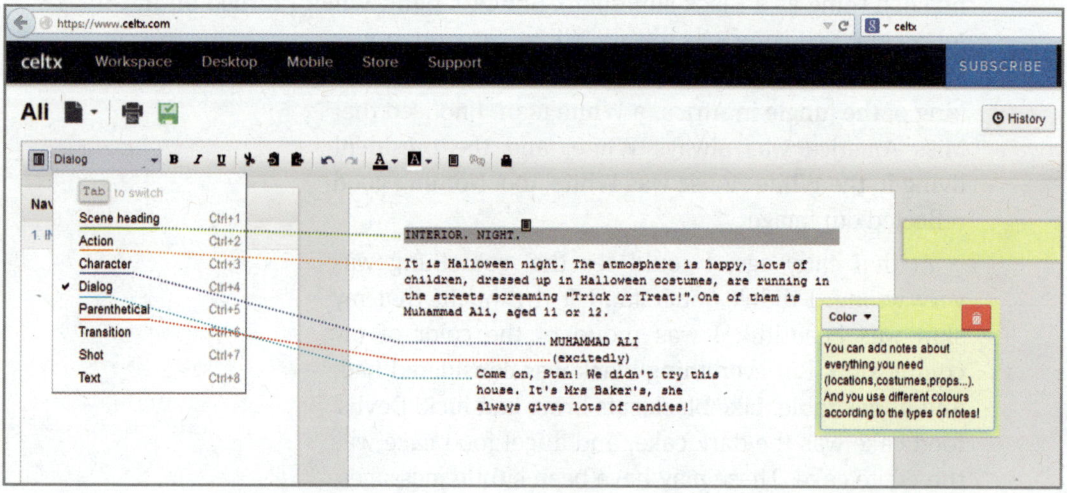

d. In order to express Ali's feelings, you can turn part of the text into a first-person speech.

- **Decide where you will start:**
  "I didn't know how...» (l. 20) or *"I thought boxing...."* (l. 25)?

- **Think about the elements you will have to change.**

e. g.

I **didn't** know how, but I **knew** that I **was** going to help my people.	→	I **don't** know how, but I **know** I'**m** going to help my people.

- **Think about how you could make the speech more powerful.**

using → *powerful words*
using → *repetitions*
using → *simple sentences*

e. **Now write a draft with your group.**

If you can, create a free account on www.celtx.com to type your script and add all the necessary notes (location, costumes…). You even have the possibility to create a collaborative account, so that each member of your team can share the same account!

tip
Tu peux utiliser la page *How to write a draft* → Textbook p. 82.

Training Task

→ Textbook p. 27

Write a passage from Ali's autobiography.

- **Watch the scene again.** What episode are you interested in?

....

....

- **Identify Muhammad Ali's feelings in this episode.**

....

....

- **Imagine how Ali could have told this episode in his autobiography.**
  You can use the text on page 25 and change certain elements.
  For example:

When	Who	What	Where
One Halloween	*a little Black girl*	*was trick-or-treating*	*around the neighborhood*
One day	*I*	*was with my dad*	*in a bus…*

Words

1 ***Words to remember*** **Vérifie que tu connais le vocabulaire du chapitre.** → Textbook p. 29

CINEMA

Impressions

① .... ② ....

....

③ ....

The actors were...

....

....

④ 🇫🇷 *effrayant* = 🇬🇧 ....

⑤ *émouvant* = ...

⑥ *cliché* = ...

⑦ *à mourir de rire* = ...

⑧ *divertissant* = ...

Cast and crew

⑨  = ...

⑩  = ...

⑪  = ...

⑫ .... = he/she provides the money for a movie

Film genres

⑬ A film = a .... = a ....

⑭

The film is a...

.... ↖ ↗ ....

.... ← The film is a... → ....

↓ ....

Plot/Scenario

⑮ It ends with ≠ ....

⑯ At the beginning... ≠ ....

⑰ The film shows... = The film ....

❷ À quels genres appartiennent ces films ? Regarde sur IMDb au besoin.

1. *Hunger Games:* ....

2. *X-men:* ....

3. *American Pie:* ....

4. *Scream:* ....

5. *Madagascar:* ....

6. *Twilight:* ....

3 **À la sortie du cinéma, imagine ce que ces spectateurs ont pu dire :**

4 **Parle de ton film préféré. Donne un maximum d'informations sur le film : genre / acteurs / réalisateur… et donne ton point de vue pour convaincre tes camarades d'aller voir le film.**

Grammar

1. LES PRONOMS RELATIFS

Les pronoms relatifs sujets : *who* et *which*

a. Dans les phrases ci-dessous, les pronoms relatifs sont en vert. Entoure en rouge les antécédents (ce qui vient avant le pronom) :

A. *Biopics are films which are based on the lives of real people.*
B. *It's the story of John Lennon who was a famous singer.*

b. Dans quelle phrase l'antécédent est-il : humain ? .... non-humain ? ......

c. Traduis maintenant ces phrases en français :

A. ....

B. ....

d. Que remarques-tu quant à la traduction de *which* et de *who* ?

....

Le pronom relatif complément d'objet : Ø

a. Dans les phrases ci-dessous, entoure en rouge les antécédents du pronom relatif Ø :

C. *The movie Ø I saw with my brother is a biopic.*
D. *The man Ø you talked to yesterday is very famous in Italy.*

b. Dans quelle phrase l'antécédent est-il : humain ? .... non-humain ? ......

c. Traduis maintenant ces phrases en français :

C. ....

D. ....

d. Que remarques-tu quant à l'utilisation du pronom relatif complément Ø ?

....

Le pronom relatif complément : *whose*

a. Lis la phrase complexe suivante :

It is the story of a man whose family immigrated in 1908.

b. L'énoncé ci-dessus a été transformé en deux phrases simples. Complète la deuxième phrase à l'aide d'un seul mot :

It is the story of a man. .... family immigrated in 1908.

c. Qu'en déduis-tu quant à la fonction du pronom relatif *whose* ?

....

d. Comment traduirais-tu cette phrase?

....

DÉDUIS !

1. Complète ce tableau :

Antécédent	Pronom relatif sujet	Pronom relatif complément d'objet
Humain	.... / *that*	.... / *that*
Non-humain	.... / *that*	.... / *that* / *which*

2. Lorsqu'il est complément du nom, le pronom relatif est ....

❶ Complète avec *Ø, who, that, whose, which* :

1. Meryl Streep is the only actress .... has had 18 Oscar nominations.

2. Walt Disney is a man .... cartoons are known by everybody.

3. *The Lord of the Rings* is one of the numerous films .... have been shot in New Zealand.

4. The man .... Di Caprio played in *The Wolf of Wall Street* is a corrupt stockbroker.

5. The show .... got the Emmy Award for Outstanding Drama Series this year is my favourite one!

❷ Work with a friend. Fais deviner à ton ami le titre d'un film célèbre, le nom d'un acteur et celui d'une actrice en les décrivant. Rédige tes phrases puis soumets-les à ton camarade. Trouvera-t-il la bonne réponse ?

e.g. **A film:** This film, which was released in 2014, is about a slave who was captured and sold, and whose owners were cruel. (**answer :** *12 years a slave*)

• **A film:** ....

....

Answer: ....

• **An actor:** ....

....

Answer: ....

• **An actress:** ....

....

Answer: ....

Parcours de RÉVISIONS : PRÉTÉRIT SIMPLE / *BE + -ING*

a. Lis l'énoncé suivant :

One Halloween, a little Black girl was trick-or-treating around the neighborhood, dressed up in a superhero costume, but her face was painted white. When I asked her why, she said...

b. Observe les verbes et leur formation :

• le verbe en vert = ... conjugué au .... +
le verbe auquel on ajoute ....

• les verbes en rouge =

– *was* = ...

– *asked* = ... + ...

– *said* = ...

c. Relis la première partie de la phrase et réponds aux questions :

A. *One Halloween, a little Black girl* ***was trick-or-treating*** *around the neighborhood...*

Dans cette première partie :

☐ On explique les circonstances dans lesquelles se déroule l'histoire.

☐ On évoque juste des faits, on donne des informations.

B. *... her face* ***was*** *painted white. When I* ***asked*** *her why, she* ***said****...*

Dans cette deuxième partie :

☐ On explique les circonstances dans lesquelles se déroule l'histoire.

☐ On évoque juste des faits, on donne des informations.

DÉDUIS !

Avec le Prétérit simple, l'énonciateur ....

Avec le Prétérit *Be* + *-ing*, l'énonciateur ....

3 Complète le texte suivant en conjuguant les verbes :

- **au Prétérit simple (verbes en minuscules)**
  Attention à la conjugaison du verbe : est-elle régulière ou irrégulière ?
  Attention aux formes interrogatives ou négatives : de quel auxiliaire vas-tu avoir besoin ?
- **au Prétérit en *Be* + *-ing* (verbes en majuscules)**
  Attention à la conjugaison de l'auxiliaire *Be* : accorde-le bien avec le sujet.

A long time ago, a superhero called Superman ....be born.......... in the city of Metropolis. He ....not have.......... superpowers when he ....be.......... a child, but as he ....grow up.........., he ....become.......... aware that he ....be.......... different. Crime ....INCREASE.......... dramatically in Metropolis when he ....decide.......... to help people.
While criminals ....STEAL.......... money from innocent people, Superman ....FIGHT.......... to free Metropolis from those criminals.

4 Complète les citations extraites de l'autobiographie de Mohammed Ali en conjuguant les verbes au Prétérit simple ou au Prétérit en *Be* + *-ing* :

1. "I ....learn.......... a lot from my parents while I ....grow up.........."
2. "My daughters Hana and Laila ....walk.......... into the hotel room where my wife, Lonnie, and I ....stay.......... in Los Angeles; Asaad ....play.......... with his mother on the bed."
3. "Someone ....direct.......... me down to the gym run by a local policeman named Joe Martin, who ....teach.......... young boys to box in his spare time."

4. "When I .... look up .... to see who I .... fight ...., my eyes widened."

2. DISCOURS DIRECT / INDIRECT

(One of my first encounters with prejudice happened when I was too young to remember, but I've heard my mother tell the story. She and I were standing at a bus stop). It was a hot day and I was thirsty, so we walked up the block to a small diner, where she asked if she could have a cup of water for her son. The man said he could not help us and closed the door in our faces.

The Soul of a Butterfly, Muhammad Ali, *2004*. ❶

a. Lis l'extrait ci-contre et le dialogue inspiré de ce texte :

Ali : "Mum, I'm thirsty"
His mother: "Could I have a cup of water for my son?"
The man: "Sorry, I can't help you". ❷

b. Repère dans le texte les phrases correspondant au dialogue.

- Quel verbe permet d'introduire la question *"Could I have a cup of water for my son?"*?

....

- Quel le verbe permet d'introduire la phrase *"Sorry, I can't help you"*?

....

c. Entoure en rouge :

- les verbes du dialogue ❷ ;
- les verbes correspondants dans le texte ❶.

d. Complète ensuite les phrases ci-dessous :

"I'm thirsty" = ... au discours indirect

"I can't [...]" = ... au discours indirect

Connais-tu un autre modal qui se termine en *-ld* ? ....
-d est la marque du passé, que tu connais dans le *-(e)d* du Prétérit.

Tu peux en déduire que *would* est le Prétérit de ....

ATTENTION

Could dans la deuxième phrase reste *could* au discours indirect. En effet, cette forme correspond à une formule de politesse.

e. Souligne en vert dans le dialogue ② les déterminants possessifs et les pronoms. Note-les dans le tableau ci-dessous ; que deviennent-ils au discours indirect ?

Discours direct ②	Discours indirect ①

f. Observe les phrases suivantes : quel est l'ordre des mots ?

- au discours direct :

Could	*I*	*have*	*a cup of water for my son?*
. . . .	. . . .	. . . .	. . . .

- au discours indirect :

She asked if	*she*	*could*	*have*	*a cup of water for my son.*
	. . . .	. . . .	. . . .	. . . .

Au discours indirect, l'ordre des mots ☐ change ☐ reste le même.

Le point d'interrogation . . . .

DÉDUIS !

- Complète le tableau ci dessous sur les changements de temps au discours indirect.

Discours direct	Discours indirect introduit par un verbe au Prétérit
Présent simple →	
"I'm fine" →	*She said that ...*
Prétérit simple →	
"I was fine" →	
Présent *Have* + participe passé →	
"I've met him" →	

Par conséquent, au discours indirect introduit par un verbe au Prétérit, *can* deviendra . . . . , *will* deviendra . . . .

- Au discours indirect, les déterminants possessifs et les pronoms
  ☐ changent ☐ restent les mêmes.
- Dans les questions au discours indirect, l'ordre des mots
  ☐ respecte l'ordre des mots d'une question ☐ retrouve l'ordre d'une phrase affirmative.

5 Complète les phrases avec *said, told* ou *asked* :

1. Mike Tyson . . . . Ali that his goal was to be the best boxer in the world.

2. My parents . . . . me if I wanted to go to the movies.

3. Martin Scorsese . . . . his best films were biopics.

4. The director . . . . his actors to be more convincing.

5. My friend . . . . the class her favorite actor was Johnny Depp.

6 Complète les phrases dans le tableau avec les déterminants possessifs ou les pronoms correspondants :

Discours direct	Discours indirect
"I'm going to the movies with my friends on Saturday." Jane said	Jane said . . . . was going to the movies with . . . . friends on Saturday.
"Our favorite film is *Raging Bull*" The twins said	The twins said . . . . favorite film was Raging Bull.
His parents to John: "We don't want you to watch this film."	His parents told John . . . . didn't want . . . . to watch this film.

7 Complète les phrases au discours indirect. Attention à conjuguer les verbes en respectant la concordance des temps.

1. Mary: "I love *Avatar*!" → She said she . . . . *Avatar*.

2. John: "Did you watch *Diana* on TV last night?" → John asked me if I . . . . *Diana* on TV the night before.

3. James: "I have never seen any biopic." → James said he . . . . any biopic.

4. Emily: "Sorry Erik, I can't talk now, I'm watching a film." → Emily told Erik she . . . . talk now, she . . . . a film.

8 Mets les phrases suivantes issues du film *Ali* au discours indirect en veillant à bien choisir les verbes introducteurs :

1. Sonny Liston to Muhammad Ali: "I am going to bust you up."

. . . .

. . . .

2. Malcolm X to the Blacks in the audience: "We don't teach you to turn the other cheek."

. . . .

. . . .

3. Malcolm X to the crowd: "Your times will never get better unless you make them better"

. . . .

. . . .

Pronunciation

1 a. Tous ces mots commencent par un [h], mais il n'est pas toujours prononcé. Écoute et coche la bonne prononciation. track 12

	☑	☒
Halloween		
help		
hero		
how		
hate		

	☑	☒
horror film		
hit		
hurricane		
hotel		

b. À l'aide d'un dictionnaire anglais, transcris les mots suivants en phonétique ci-dessous :

1. help /. . . . . / **2.** hour /. . . . . /

→ Comment peux-tu savoir si le [h] se prononce ou pas ?

c. Vérifie dans un dictionnaire en ligne la prononciation des termes suivants :

habit – hungry – honor – hot – heavy – his – hour – headache – head – honest – hand – him

2 Écoute maintenant les phrases suivantes, en faisant attention à la prononciation du [h] dans les mots soulignés : track 13

Her biopic has been seen by a lot of people. It is the real story of her life, even if some parts have been changed a little, but her love affair with her American friend was real. She lived with him for a long time, then they finally broke up.

Que remarques-tu ?

☐ Le [h] est toujours prononcé. ☐ Le [h] n'est pas toujours prononcé.

3 Quelle conclusion en tires-tu ?

- Les mots lexicaux commençant par la lettre [h] se prononcent avec le son /. . . . . / qui doit être bien prononcé.
- Le [h] de certains mots comme *heir, honor, honest* et *hour* . . . .
- Généralement, quand il est au début d'un mot grammatical, le [h] . . . .

How to...

...read a text *and not panic!*

Entraîne-toi 1

Lis le texte suivant. Les mots de vocabulaire les plus difficiles ont été floutés afin que tu ne t'en préoccupes pas, dans un premier temps. Tu vas voir qu'ils ne sont pas indispensables à la compréhension globale du texte.

From cycling to boxing

When it was time to go home, I discovered my bike was gone. I was so [illegible] I went looking for the police to report it. Someone directed me down to the gym run by a local policeman named Joe Martin, who was teaching young boys to box [illegible]. I told Mr. Martin that I was gonna [illegible] whoever stole my bike. I was half crying and probably didn't look too convincing. I remember Mr. Martin telling me, "Well, you better learn how to fight before you start challenging people that you're gonna [illegible]."

The Soul of a Butterfly, Muhammad Ali, Hana Yasmeen Ali, 2004

❶ **a. Avant de lire le texte en entier, prépare-toi à la lecture pour deviner ce dont il sera question. Regarde bien les éléments suivants. Qu'en comprends-tu ?**

le titre de l'œuvre | *le titre du chapitre, ou du passage* | *l'auteur* | *la première phrase*

....

....

....

b. Imagine en quelques mots ce dont il sera question dans le texte :

....

....

Entraîne-toi 2

❷ **a. Lis le reste du paragraphe une fois, sans rien faire d'autre que te laisser porter par les mots. Qu'as-tu compris à ce stade ?**

....

....

b. Maintenant, lis le texte à nouveau et souligne les mots qui te semblent importants par rapport au titre et à la première phrase du texte. Concentre-toi sur ces mots pour comprendre plus d'éléments. Qu'as-tu compris à ce stade ?

....

....

❸ **Concentre-toi sur les noms propres :**

- Identifie ceux qui désignent des personnes et souligne-les dans une autre couleur.
- Entoure le verbe qui désigne ce que chaque personne fait et relis-le à la personne.

Entraîne-toi 3

❹ **Choisis une troisième couleur pour souligner les mots qui ressemblent au français, puis reporte-les ci-après.**

En t'appuyant sur le contexte, vérifie s'ils ont le même sens en français et en anglais. Si, quand tu traduis littéralement, la phrase ne veut rien dire, cela signifie que le mot anglais a un sens différent : quel est-il alors ?

Mots du texte	Sens probable
....	....
....	....
....	....
....	....
....	....
....	....
....	....
....	....

5 Fais aussi attention aux mots qui ont plusieurs significations, selon la manière dont ils sont employés.

Par exemple, tu connais sûrement le verbe *run* qui signifie .... comme dans la phrase *Usain Bolt runs very fast*.
Mais dans notre texte, le verbe *run* est suivi d'un complément d'objet indirect : *"by a local policeman"*. Il ne peut donc pas avoir le même sens. Lis bien le reste du texte pour deviner le sens de ce verbe…

a. Regarde les phrases qui contiennent des mots floutés. Essaye de deviner ce qui manque.

Verbe .... et adverbe *so* (qui signifie tellement). Ils sont donc sûrement suivis d'un ....

A. "When it was time to go home, I discovered my bike was gone. I was so ▒▒ I went looking for the police to report it."

Tu comprends ce qui est arrivé au narrateur, tu peux donc imaginer ce qui se cache derrière le carré gris. Fais des propositions : ....
....

Tu peux comprendre le sens de *stole* parce que tu sais ce qui est arrivé au vélo (première phrase).

B. "I told Mr. Martin that I was gonna whoever stole my bike."

Maintenant que tu sais ce que ressent le narrateur, à ton avis, qu'a-t-il envie de faire à *"whoever stole my bike"* ?

....

....

....

Décompose ce mot :

.... + ...

Puisqu'il est devant *stole*, qui est conjugué, cela signifie que ce mot a la fonction de

....

Des deux parties du mot, laquelle semble la plus importante ?

....

Imagine ce qui se cache derrière le carré gris. Fais des propositions :

....

....

b. Voici à présent le texte complet. Vérifie avec ton professeur le sens précis des mots que tu ne comprends toujours pas... s'il en reste !

From cycling to boxing

When it was time to go home, I discovered my bike was gone. I was so upset I went looking for the police to report it. Someone directed me down to the gym run by a local policeman named Joe Martin, who was teaching young boys to box in his spare time. I told Mr. Martin that I was gonna whup whoever stole my bike. I was half crying and probably didn't look too convincing. I remember Mr. Martin telling me, "Well, you better learn how to fight before you start challenging people that you're gonna whup."

The Soul of a Butterfly, Muhammad Ali, Hana Yasmeen Ali, 2004

Teste-toi !

Ce texte est la suite de celui que tu viens de lire.

(...) Joe Martin was the man who started me [redacted] in boxing, but regularly I [redacted] with a Black man named Fred Stoner, who taught me how to [redacted]. If I ever found out who took my bike, I was going to be ready. Mr. Martin produced a local television show called Tomorrow's Champions as part of the Columbia Gym's amateur program. It offered instant local celebrity status to his boxers. When I first started boxing, all I wanted was to someday buy my parents a house and [redacted] a nice big car. I [redacted] if I could turn pro and get on Saturday night fights, I could make four thousand dollars just for one night. Then my dreams started to [redacted]. When I was in school, sometimes I would pretend that they were announcing my name over the [redacted] system, saying "Cassius Clay, [redacted] champion of the world".

The Soul of a Butterfly, Muhammad Ali, Hana Yasmeen Ali, 2004

1 Applique les techniques que tu as mises en œuvre lors de la lecture de la première partie pour lire cette suite.

2 Relis maintenant l'intégralité du texte, et propose un résumé en français en quelques mots.

From cycling to boxing

When it was time to go home, I discovered my bike was gone. I was so upset I went looking for the police to report it. Someone directed me down to the gym run by a local policeman named Joe Martin, who was teaching young boys to box in his spare time. I told Mr. Martin that I was gonna whup whoever stole my bike. I was half crying and probably didn't look too convincing. I remember Mr. Martin telling me, "Well, you better learn how to fight before you start challenging people that you're gonna whup."

(...) Joe Martin was the man who started me out in boxing, but regularly I trained with a Black man named Fred Stoner, who taught me how to jab. If I ever found out who took my bike, I was going to be ready. Mr. Martin produced a local television show called Tomorrow's Champions as part of the Columbia Gym's amateur program. It offered instant local celebrity status to his boxers. When I first started boxing, all I wanted was to someday buy my parents a house and own a nice big car. I figured if I could turn pro and get on Saturday night fights, I could make four thousand dollars just for one night. Then my dreams started to grow. When I was in school, sometimes I would pretend that they were announcing my name over the loudspeaker system, saying "Cassius Clay, heavyweight champion of the world."

The Soul of a Butterfly, Muhammad Ali, Hana Yasmeen Ali, 2004

3 Street art attacks

Discover

Training Task

→ Textbook p. 37

Act out an interview with a street artist.

1 Read the following article to prepare for the interview (whatever role you are playing!):

How to Conduct an Interview

One of the hardest skills for a young reporter to master is interviewing. It takes preparation and persistence to conduct a good interview. Follow these steps and learn how to interview like a pro!

STEP 1: Brainstorm a list of questions.

The more specific your questions are, the better! And never ask questions that can be answered with a simple yes or no. Make your interviewee talk!

Be sure to write all your questions down in a notebook, then practise asking them with a partner.

STEP 2: Come prepared with:

- A notebook
- A recording device (always ask permission before recording an interview)

STEP 3: Conduct your interview in an organized, timely manner.

During the interview:

- Be courteous to your subject.
- Always take time to ask for an explanation about things you don't understand.

Always listen carefully to the answers. Each answer could lead to more questions or include an answer to a question you haven't asked yet.

STEP 4: Even if you are recording an interview, take notes.

Don't try to write every word said. It will slow down the interview. Just take down the highlights.

At home, expand your notes by following up on things you learned in your interview with more research!

www.scholastic.com

2 **Fill in the following table to prepare your interview.**

Conducting the interview	Journalist → Prepare your questions	Artist → Prepare your answers
Introductory questions: "Can you tell me about yourself...?" (age, origin, hobbies...)		
Specific questions: • Motives • Inspiration • Techniques		
Follow up questions: "What did you mean...?" "Can you give me more details...?"		

Understand

Should it stay or should it go?

→ Textbook p. 38

2 Need help?

a. **The first paragraph often sums up the main facts. Underline the key information.**

b. **The first sentence of each paragraph introduces a new idea. Underline and read all the first sentences – you now have a clear idea of the whole article.**

I'm the Accidental Owner of a Banksy

By Cara Tabachnick | 10/18/2013 at 3:04 PM

"Are you going to be rich?" That is the first question people ask me upon finding out that in the morning hours of October 17, the famed street artist Banksy painted a mural on the side of a building my family owns in East Williamsburg.

The truth is – at the end of an exhausting day filled with phone calls talking to lawyers, security companies, art experts, and reporters – I have no idea what it means. There is no rulebook when one of the most famous artists in the world decides to drop his work into your life.

The painting on our building was the seventeenth piece of art to appear during Banksy's monthlong tour in New York. Each day, the shadowy London-based graffiti artist leaves behind a work of art somewhere in the city. The two prior days had witnessed the appearance of a small silhouette of the Twin Towers spray-painted on a wall in Tribeca and a sculpture of an expectant Ronald McDonald getting his shoes shined by a real human being in the South Bronx.

Mayor Bloomberg[1] has promised to paint over any Banksy pieces on city property and has labeled him a vandal. "You running up to somebody's property or public property and defacing it is not my definition of art," he told the reporters on Wednesday. The NYPD has promised to charge[2] him – if they can find him.

I had been following the Banksy phenomenon with mild interest (my husband is a fan), but had no idea what was in store for our family when my father texted me yesterday morning, "Banksy painted our building last night and a huge crowd is forming. What should we do?"(...)

Should we preserve it immediately? Do we have a public duty to do so? How does one preserve a piece of art like this? How do we control the crowds with gawkers and fans of the elusive[3] artist, many of them foreign tourists, who were suddenly standing outside the building? Will it make us money? (...)

It's hard to know what the future holds. In England, where many of his pieces survive, buildings have gained value and local governments take great pride in his work. As the cult of Banksy grows, that could mean tour groups coming around to look at the painting. It is hard for our family to envision busloads of tourists being dropped off at our front door every day. But it is a possibility.

nymag.com

1. Mayor of the City of New York (2001 – 2013) – **2.** to officially accuse somebody of a crime – **3.** hard to find or capture

c. Now read the whole article and pick out the following information.

Facts
- *Place*
- *Date*
- *Event*

People involved
- *Private citizens*
- *Artist*
- *Professionals*
- *Officials*

Their reactions

TOOLS

Reactions

☹ • Irritaded • Furious

😐 • Puzzled • Embarrassed

☺ • Enthusiastic • Thrilled

Training Task

→ Textbook p. 39

Street artist *vs* building owner.

Prepare what you will say.

Street artist → think of:

- What you painted: ....
- Your intention: ....

....

....

- Prepare for all possibilities! What will you say if:

the New Yorker loves your work and wants to keep it

the New Yorker loves your work and wants to sell it

the New Yorker hates your job and wants to call the police...

....

....

....

....

New Yorker → think of:

- Your age: .... • Your job: ....
- Your opinion about graffiti: ....

....

....

- Your reactions to the street artist's mural on your building and what you will tell him/her: ....

....

....

....

Final tasks

Will you sign the petition? Explain why or why not.

→ Textbook p. 40

A wall for street artists

I am starting this petition in the hope that Medway Council will be kind enough to construct designated walls for street artists in the Medway Towns. The problem I see is that public people don't appreciate graffiti as art, and see it as mindless vandalism. Yet speaking to street artists and various creative people, it is more a way of expressing themselves visually.

Admittedly there is a type of graffiti known as tags or tagging in which the artist isn't necessarily looking for a visually pleasing piece of art – the goal in tagging is to get your tag in as many places as possible. But the majority of street artists only want to create a piece of art that holds a message or meaning, and most of the time it is aimed at making things better for the people and the planet.

Building a designated wall, I believe, will considerably improve the unwanted vandalism. Instead of artists having to illegally spread their art on private walls (thus creating a conflict between artist and non-artist), it will create a place for people to freely express their work and appreciate others.

This project will only be able to go ahead if many different people sign this petition and show their views and opinions.

We cannot do this without you! Thank you so much!

• **Will you sign the petition? If you will, forward it to a friend. If you won't, reply to the sender. Explain your point of view.**

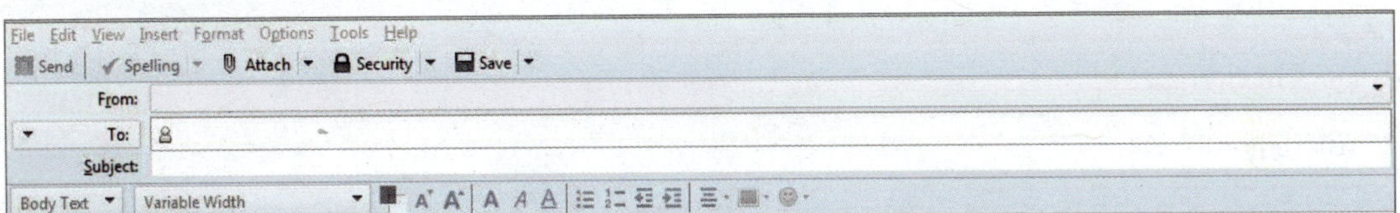

. . . .

. . . .

. . . .

. . . .

. . . .

. . . .

Words

1 *Words to remember* **Vérifie que tu connais le vocabulaire du chapitre.** → Textbook p. 41

TALKING ART

Agreeing and disagreeing

Tu participes à un débat. Trouve trois façons de dire que :

- tu es d'accord avec ce qui vient d'être dit :

① ....

② ....

③ ....

- tu n'es pas d'accord :

④ ....

⑤ ....

⑥ ....

Appreciation

⑦ Colourful ≠ ....

⑧ Cheeky = ...

⑨ *provocant* = ...

⑩ *prétentieux* = ...

Selon toi, quelle réalisation de *Street art* illustre chacun de ces adjectifs :

⑪ Witty ....

⑫ Cheeky ....

⑬ Ugly ....

Reactions

⑭ ....

⑯ ....

⑱ ....

⑮ ....

⑰ ....

⑲ ....

2 Barre l'intrus et propose un autre mot qui aille avec les autres :

1. stencil – sculpture – spray paint – wall: . . . .

2. aggressive – funny – shocking – ugly: . . . .

3. criticize – accuse – praise – condemn: . . . .

3 Complète les phrases suivantes avec des adjectifs de la rubrique *Appreciation* :

1. Banksy drew a . . . . image of a child working in a factory, on the wall of a supermarket.

2. He paints . . . . graffiti, which sometimes shock people.

3. The artworks I saw are rather . . . . and did not impress me.

4. The sentence written on the wall was rather . . . . and made me smile.

Grammar

1. PRÉPOSITIONS + V *-ING*

a. Observe les énoncés suivants :

A. *How did you get **into** doing street art?*

B. *We decided **against** giving street artists a wall.*

C. *The effect **of** building a designated wall for street artists will reduce acts of vandalism.*

D. *The goal **in** tagging is **to** get your tag in as many places as possible.*

Les mots en **bleu** sont des ☐ articles ☐ prépositions ☐ pronoms.

De quel mot est suivi chacun de ces mots en **bleu** ?

- en **A** : . . . . (formation : verbe . . . . + ...)
- en **B** : . . . . (formation : verbe . . . . + ...)
- en **C** : . . . . (formation : verbe . . . . + ...)
- en **D** : . . . . (formation : verbe . . . . + ...)

L'ajout de la terminaison . . . . . à chacun des verbes transforme ceux-ci en . . . .

b. Souligne les deux autres prépositions dans l'énoncé C. De quoi sont-elles suivies ?

- La préposition .... est suivie ☐ d'un nom ☐ d'un verbe.
- La préposition .... est suivie ☐ d'un nom ☐ d'un verbe.

c. Dans l'énoncé D :

- Qu'exprime *to* dans *"to get your tag in as many places as possible"* ?

....

- Quelle est la forme du verbe après *to* ?

....

d. Et les prépositions ?

Réfléchis au sens des prépositions (en te servant éventuellement du précis p. 155 de ton manuel). En fonction de leur sens, déduis celui des phrases du a. Reformule-les en français.

A. ....

B. ....

C. ....

D. ....

DÉDUIS !

Une préposition est suivie :

- soit d'un nom ;
- soit d'un verbe transformé en nom. Dans ce cas, c'est l'ajout de .... à la base verbale qui permet de transformer le verbe en nom.

ATTENTION

Quand *to* exprime le but, il est suivi de la base verbale ☐ avec ☐ sans *-ing*.

1 Mets les verbes entre parenthèses à la forme adéquate :

1. He is only good at .... point a finger at .... artists.

2. Banksy was never arrested for .... deface .... public property.

3. Can he .... appreciate .... art without .... criticize .... it?

4. I am thinking of .... sign .... the petition.

5. To me, ...skateboard........ is really about ....have fun........ .

6. Shepard Fairey actually got into ......do...... street art to ......express...... himself.

2 **Complète les phrases avec la préposition qui convient... Attention, il y en a une en trop !**

against – about – for – to

1. Punk rock is mostly .... rebelling against the establishment.

2. Londoners signed a petition .... the removal of a Banksy graffiti.

3. The artist became famous .... spray-painting a gigantic roller skater on a wall in Brick Lane.

2. EXPRIMER UN POINT DE VUE AVEC *WILL, MAY, SHOULD...*

a. Lis les énoncés suivants et souligne les groupes verbaux. De quel type de mot les auxiliaires modaux (en bleu) sont-ils suivis ? ....

A. *I don't know what to do... If we leave Bansky's graffiti, some people **may** try to steal our wall!*

B. *You **should** preserve this piece of art, I mean, that's what I would do!*

C. *You are so lucky! You **will** become rich!*

b. Dans quel énoncé donne-t-on un conseil ? ☐ A ☐ B ☐ C

c. Dans quel énoncé exprime-t-on une probabilité ? ☐ A ☐ B ☐ C

d. Dans quel énoncé exprime-t-on une certitude ? ☐ A ☐ B ☐ C

DÉDUIS !

Les auxiliaires modaux sont suivis d'un verbe à la forme ....

1. Le modal .... peut permettre d'exprimer le conseil.
2. Le modal .... peut permettre d'exprimer la probabilité.
3. Le modal .... peut permettre d'exprimer la certitude.

3 **Complète les phrases suivantes avec *should, may* ou *will* :**

1. The mayor of New York City .... be more tolerant with graffiti.

2. Banksy .... put up another piece in New York tomorrow.

3. Our street .... be defaced if we say nothing.

4. I want to become a graffiti artist but my parents .... disapprove.

5. What .... we do with these ugly graffiti?

4 Joue à Madame Irma avec ton voisin !

Prédis son avenir (travail, brevet, santé, amour, gloire et beauté !). Mais attention, module ce que tu vas lui dire en fonction de ton degré de certitude, et conseille-le bien sûr :-)

e.g. I *see here that you may become very famous if you...*

Pronunciation

1 La prononciation des mots en *-age* **track 17**

a. Dans ce chapitre sur le *Street Art*, tu as utilisé un certain nombre de mots se terminant par *-age*. Écoute les mots suivants, puis répète-les :

damage – image – message – page – village – age – marriage – advantage

b. Transcris les mots ci-dessous, en faisant bien attention à la prononciation de *-age*.

1. Damage / .... /	**5.** Village / .... /
2. Image / .... /	**6.** Age / .... /
3. Message / .... /	**7.** Marriage / .... /
4. Page / .... /	**8.** Advantage / .... /

c. Dans les mots ci-dessus, *-age* se prononce-t-il toujours de la même façon ? ☐ oui ☐ non.

d. Quelle conclusion en tires-tu ?

Dans les mots d'une seule syllabe, *-age* se prononce /......./ car cette syllabe est forcément accentuée.

Dans les mots de plus d'une syllabe, *-age* se prononce généralement /......./ ou /......./, car *-age* est généralement inaccentué.

e. Connais-tu d'autres mots anglais se terminant par *-age* ?

Note-les ci-dessous, et indique la prononciation de *-age* en appliquant la règle que tu viens de voir :

....

....

....

....

2 La prononciation des mots en *-ace* track 18

a. La même règle est valable pour les noms se terminant par *-ace*. Transcris les mots suivants en appliquant la règle que tu viens de voir :

1. Menace / .... /

2. Necklace / .... /

3. Face / .... /

4. Race / .... /

5. Palace / .... /

6. Place / .... /

7. Surface / .... /

8. Terrace / .... /

b. Écoute et répète ces mots, en vérifiant que tu les as bien transcrits.

4 Breaking the news

Discover

Fact or fiction?

→ Textbook p. 48

1 b. Need help? **Read the headlines and underline in different colours:**

- the words that refer to places, the words that refer to natural catastrophes, the verbs that refer to the consequences of these catastrophes.

STATE OF EMERGENCY
IN NEW YORK AFTER SUPERSTORM FLOODS THE CITY

6.8 magnitude earthquake strikes New Zealand

STORM ALERT
Hurricane Katrina could be catastrophic

California wildfire destroys 68 homes

2 a. Listen to the news flashes and take notes.

News flashes	Notes
A.	....
B.	....
C.	....
D.	....

b. Organize your notes.

News flashes	Type of disaster	Places mentioned	Consequences	Corresponding picture
A.				
B.				
C.				
D.				

Breaking news

→ Textbook p. 49

4 a. Do you think the TV reporter did a good job? Circle 👍 or 👎 in the tutorial below.

b. Explain your opinion, and make suggestions for improving the news report.

COVERING DISASTERS AND ACCIDENTS

Accidents and disasters – everything from plane and train crashes to earthquakes, tornadoes and tsunamis – are some of the hardest stories to cover.
Here are some tips to keep in mind when covering such events.

Get Plenty of Description

Readers will want to know what the scene of the disaster looked like, sounded like, smelled like. Get the sights, sounds and smells in your notes. Think of yourself as a camera, recording every visual detail you can.

👍 👎 ....

....

Find The Officials in Charge

In the aftermath of a disaster there will usually be dozens of emergency responders on the scene – firefighters, police, EMTs, and so on. Find the person who's in charge of the emergency response.

👍 👎 ....

....

Get Eyewitness Accounts

Information from emergency authorities is great, but you need to also get quotes from people who were there and saw with their own eyes what happened.

👍 👎 ....

....

Find The Heroes

In nearly every disaster there are heroes who emerge – people who bravely and selflessly jeopardize their own safety in order to rescue or help others. Find those people and interview them.

👍 👎 ....

....

Get The Numbers

Disaster stories are often about numbers – how many people were killed or injured, how much property was destroyed, how fast the plane was traveling, etc. Remember to gather these for your story.

👍 👎 ....

....

journalism.about.com, Tony Rogers

Training Task

→ Textbook p. 49

Take part in a newsflash.

1 Read this piece of news:

Hurricane Sandy: high winds and flooding hit US east coast

President Barack Obama has warned of a "big and powerful storm". In a briefing at the White House, he warned residents up and down the US east coast [...] to take Sandy seriously. Significant flooding has already been reported. The public safety director for Atlantic City said much of the city is underwater. [...] Thousands have lost power in Virginia and Maryland. Power outages have also been reported in Connecticut and Rhode Island.

The Guardian, Oct. 29 2012

a. Identify the type of disaster: . . . .

b. Pick out the following information:

Location	Damage	Victims	Fighting the flood

❷ Imagine you are involved in the event.

a. Choose your role:

☐ *President Obama* ☐ *a resident* ☐ *a victim* ☐ *a rescuer / a firefighter* ☐ *an official*
☐ *a reporter* ☐ *other:* . . . .

b. Pick useful phrases according to your role:

☐ *"We're live from..."*
☐ *"I've lived here all my life..."*
☐ *"I'm standing here today with..."*
☐ *"This is the worst... in years."*
☐ *"The story is changing rapidly..."*
☐ *"My fellow Americans..."*
☐ *"I'm now declaring a state of emergency."*
☐ *"Good evening ladies and gentlemen."*
☐ *"This is news at ... and I'm ..."*
☐ *"Back to you in the studio..."*
☐ *"Officials say..."*
☐ *"Take a live look behind me."*
☐ *"I've never seen anything like this..."*
☐ *"As you can see..."*

c. Decide what you will say:

. . . .
. . . .
. . . .
. . . .

Understand

To bee or not to bee

→ Textbook p. 50

A is for Acid Rain, B is for Bee

You never went out on rainy days. Health and safety wouldn't let you. Instead you played games online, or read books, or talked to your friends on your smartie, or even watched a movie – they still had live movies in those days, before ceegee took over for good (so much safer than real life, of course, but somehow not as exciting). In those days before the Cloud, you actually still *went* to school, instead of doing it all from home, and friends were people you saw every day, and games were what you played outside – that is, if it wasn't raining.

In a minute. Come here first. I hardly ever see you, kid. Yes, that's right. Climb onto my knee. Let me tell you a story. What about? Well, let me see. Do you like animals? No, *not* ceegee animals. I mean actual, real-life animals. Tigers and elephants and whales and such.

No kid, I've never seen a tiger. [...] Let me tell you about the bee. It was in the summer of – well, never mind. A long time ago, when I was your age. I used to go to school just round the corner, where the Parklands building is now. My school was called Saint Oswald's. Even in those days, it was pretty old. There was even an actual park nearby, with trees and grass and everything. We used to have a lot more of that in those days. Now you don't really get it much, because of the rain. And flowers too. In those days flowers grew mostly *outside*.

That was where the bees came in. Of course, they were pretty rare even then. People said they were dying out. Some kind of disease, or the rain, or the sun, or maybe smarties, which some people said were interfering with the special signals the bees gave out to find their way back to where they lived. [...]

But that day, we *all* saw the bee, Philip and Johnny and Frankie and me. For all we knew it might have been the very last bee in the whole world. In any case, we never saw another one after that, and by the time I left school, the park was gone to make way for these apartment blocks.

J. Harris, "A is for Acid Rain, B is for Bee",
in *Beacons: Stories of our not so distant future*, 2013.

2 b. Underline in two different colours:

- the references to time. What do they indicate? ....

....

- the nouns or pronouns referring to characters. What do you understand about the situation?

....

....

c. Circle the words "ceegee" and "the Cloud" in the text, and try to infer their meanings.

"No, not ceegee animals. I mean actual, real-life animals." (l. 11)

- How could you rephrase this sentence?

→ "No, not .... animals. I mean actual, real-life animals."

- Now, say "ceegee" out loud. What does it sound like? ....

Check the meaning of these letters online. ....

- The narrator say "the Cloud" and not "a cloud". What does it say about this "Cloud"?

....

....

d. What is the world like in this story? Pick out elements from the text.

	Leisure	Animals	School	Climate
"Before the Cloud"				
"Now"				

Training Task

→ Textbook p. 51

You're a "cli-fi" writer... Need help?

1 Choose your starting point.

Look at each ✍ and read what comes just before: this is what you will have to develop. Before choosing a starting point, make sure you understand what each passage is about. Here are possible beginnings for you:

"You never went out on rainy days. Health and safety wouldn't let you."

→ *They thought it was too dangerous because...*

"...and games were what you played outside – that is, if it wasn't raining."

→ *Because when it was raining, we had to stay indoors...*

"In those days flowers grew mostly outside."

→ *And animals also lived outside...*

2 Develop your story.

Think about what you want to explain in your short addition. These questions may help:

"You never went out on rainy days. Health and safety wouldn't let you."

- What is Health and Safety?
- What other future institutions can you imagine?
- What do you imagine will be forbidden in the future?

"...and games were what you played outside – that is, if it wasn't raining."

- What is the problem with the rain?
- How can the climate have changed people's lives?
- What do teens do all day long if there are no longer games?

"In those days flowers grew mostly outside."

- When do you think the story takes place?
- How do you imagine the outside world?
- What happened to flowers?

3 Start writing.

Include the sentences that come just before and after your addition to make it more natural to read.

Words

1 *Words to remember* **Vérifie que tu connais le vocabulaire du chapitre.** → Textbook p. 53

DISASTER

Before a disaster

① threat *(n)* → .... *(v)*

② *urgence, situation critique* = ...

During and after

③ hit = ... ④ inundated = ...

⑤ détruire = ... / ....

Climate events

⑥ when it hasn't rained for a long time ....

⑦  = ...

⑧  = ...

⑨ Sandy or Katrina... ....

⑩ *un orage* = ...

⑪ *le réchauffement climatique* = ...

⑫ *le changement climatique* = ...

⑬ a fire that is not controlled and that can burn a large area very quickly ....

Help and rescue

⑭ a person who fights fires ....

⑮ officials = ...

⑯ .... ⑰ ....

Reactions

⑱

The situation can be...

....

⑲

People can be...

....

❷ Complète ces phrases :

1. The government declared a state of .... to deal with the damage caused by the hurricane.

2. Several flood victims were .... by firefighters.

3. The earthquake caused 20 .... and several serious injuries.

4. Fortunately the historic center suffered no serious .... in the storm.

3 Complète les titres suivants avec les éléments de ton choix :

1.
Hero .... rescues
little girl from ....

2.
Heavy rains in Hampshire
result in ....

3.
....
said to increase the number of hurricanes
in the years to come

4.
STRONG WINDS .... **CITY**
CENTER. SEVERAL BUILDINGS ....

4 Complète ces témoignages de civils ou de sauveteurs ayant vécu des catastrophes.

1. "It was horrible, I mean, I was really ...."
2. "My husband and I ran to the closest shelter, and we waited there for hours. We tried to stay very .... to keep our energy."
3. "When I saw the twister in the distance, I was ...., it was very ...., I had never seen anything like it."
4. "Before going to rescue people, we always try to .... because sometimes it is really impressive."

Grammar

1. PRÉSENT *HAVE* + PARTICIPE PASSÉ (2)

a. Lis les énoncés suivants :

A. *Yesterday, a storm **destroyed** a village in the USA; people were terrified.*

B. In 2002, a hurricane ***struck*** Louisiana and ***flooded*** my school.

Ils sont conjugués au . . . .

→ Forme des verbes en gras : *destroyed/flooded* : base verbale + ...

struck : . . . .

C. *A flood has just devastated New York, and people are still very shocked.*

D. *A hurricane has struck Louisiana; a lot of people are injured, and the damages are heavy.*

→ Composition des verbes en gras : . . . . + ...

Quelle est la conjugaison de ce premier mot ? ☐ Présent ☐ Prétérit

Qu'est-ce que cela indique à propos de la forme en elle-même ?

. . . .

b. Entoure les indications de temps dans les énoncés A et B. Elles renvoient au :
☐ présent ☐ passé.

L'énonciateur évoque donc : ☐ la situation présente ☐ des événements passés.

c. Dans les énoncés C et D, regarde les verbes soulignés. Ils sont conjugués au :
☐ Présent ☐ Prétérit.

On peut donc en déduire que l'énonciateur s'intéresse au ☐ présent ☐ passé.

Pourquoi les verbes en gras sont-ils conjugués différemment ?

. . . .

Ils désignent des événements ☐ qui se produisent en ce moment ☐ qui se sont déjà produits.

DÉDUIS !

En utilisant le Présent *Have* + participe passé, l'énonciateur parle de faits ☐ passés ☐ présents, mais ce qui l'intéresse c'est le moment . . . .
Il fait un constat, un état des lieux.

À l'inverse, en utilisant le Prétérit, l'énonciateur parle bien toujours de faits . . . . ,
mais il s'intéresse aux faits en eux-mêmes, pas à leurs conséquences sur le moment de parole.

1 Pour chaque énoncé, choisis la forme qui convient : Prétérit ou *Have* au Présent + participe passé ?

1. My mother ☐ just arrived ☐ has just arrived from a flooded city. She looks exhausted.

2. Twenty years ago, there ☐ were ☐ have been fewer hurricanes.

3. Look at that! The flood ☐ destroy ☐ has destroyed the city!

4. Strong winds ☐ devastated ☐ have devastated the city center. You really can't go out!

5. In the 1950s, global warming ☐ did not exist ☐ has not existed and few victims ☐ were recorded ☐ have been recorded.

2 Conjugue les verbes du texte suivant, en choisissant soit le Prétérit, soit la forme *Have* au Présent + participe passé. Fais attention aux verbes irréguliers (si tu as un doute, consulte le précis grammatical p. 173) :

When the rescue team .... arrive ...., they .... find .... a lot of damage and .... have .... to rescue dozens of victims. The conditions .... be .... really hard with strong blasts of wind and still some heavy rain. Today, when I look at this same spot, I can hardly believe it .... happen .... here because everything .... change .... : the trees and flower .... grow .... back and the city .... repair .... all the roads and houses. They .... even / build .... an earthquake shelter.

1 BIS. VOIX ACTIVE OU VOIX PASSIVE ?

a. Rappel. Lis cet énoncé et remémore-toi la construction de la voix passive :

This village is inundated: its inhabitants were evacuated yesterday night.

Formation : auxiliaire .... (conjugué) + ... du verbe

b. Lis les deux énoncés suivants et souligne :

– en rouge l'auxiliaire de la voix passive ;
– en bleu le verbe.

A. *For the last eight days, Muchelney **has been cut off** from the world.*
B. *You get very cross because nothing **has been done**.*

c. Observe attentivement comment cet assemblage est formé, et complète le schéma :

*Muchelney **has been cut off** from the world.*

. . . .

d. Comment est conjugué le verbe à la voix active ?

C. *You've already just finished the renovation.*

. . . .

e. Entoure les sujets des énoncés A, B et C. Quel élément est mis en avant en :

A. ☐ le village de Muchelney / ☐ la catastrophe naturelle

B. ☐ l'absence d'initiative / ☐ les autorités

C. ☐ le sujet *you* / la personne interrogée / ☐ les travaux de remise en état

DÉDUIS !

Dans une phrase, c'est toujours le . . . . qui est mis en avant. Le choix du sujet, et ce que l'on veut dire, entraînera selon les cas le choix de la voix active ou de la voix passive.

Formation :

- **Présent *Have* + participe passé (voix active) :**

Sujet + auxiliaire . . . . (Présent) + ... du verbe.

- **Présent *Have* + Participe passé (voix passive) :**

Sujet + auxiliaire . . . . (Présent) + *been* + ... du verbe.

3 À partir des photos suivantes, fais le bilan des réparations. Attention au choix de la voix !

1.

Before

Now

TOOLS

- wreckage / debris
- electric pole
- pavement / track
- remove / clear
- clean up
- fix / repair / rebuild

. . . .

. . . .

2.

Before

Now

. . . .

. . . .

3.

Before

Now

. . . .

. . . .

4 Imagine ce qui a pu se passer et quelles sont les conséquences :

. . . .

. . . .

. . . .

. . . .

. . . .

. . . .

. . . .

. . . .

. . . .

. . . .

2. USED TO

a. Regarde les énoncés suivants :

A. *I **used to go** to school just round the corner, where the Parklands building is now.*

B. *I **went** to school with your cousin yesterday.*

C. *We **used to see** bees all around the world for many years, but they are dying out now.*

D. *We **saw** bees in the house three days ago.*

b. Observe les formes verbales en gras :

- Dans les énoncés **A** et **C**, les verbes **en bleu** sont à la forme . . . .

Ils sont précédés de l'expression . . . . qui est conjuguée au . . . .

- Dans les énoncés **B** et **D**, les verbes **en rouge** sont conjugués au . . . .

c. Observe les segments soulignés :

- À quel moment renvoient ceux de **A** et **C** ? ☐ présent ☐ passé

  ceux de **B** et **D** ? ☐ présent ☐ passé

- Que nous indique chacun de ces segments concernant l'école (en **A**) et les abeilles (en **C**) ?

DÉDUIS !

- La forme *used to* + verbe à l'infinitif permet à l'énonciateur de souligner, encore plus qu'avec un simple Prétérit, que l'événement passé ☐ est toujours d'actualité ☐ n'est plus du tout d'actualité (contrairement à la forme *Have* au Présent + participe passé !).
- *Used to* indique aussi que l'événement passé . . . . (c'est la valeur contenue dans *use*).
- La forme *used to* n'est donc jamais obligatoire, et peut être remplacée par un simple . . . . , tout dépend du message que l'énonciateur veut transmettre !

5 Pour chaque énoncé, choisis entre les deux formes en gras. Dans les énoncés concernés, souligne ce qui justifie d'utiliser la forme *used to* :

1. I **ran / used to run** ten kilometers every day when I was a student, but I can't anymore, I am too busy.

2. Every year, I **went / used to go** on holidays with my parents by the seaside.

3. Two days ago, Sarah **met / used to meet** John's parents for the first time.

4. Every other week, they **went / used to go** to the gym with their friends, but they are too old now.

5. One day in Australia, we **saw / used to see** an alligator and we **were / used to be** really scared.

6 Prétérit ou *used to* ? Mets le verbe à la forme qui convient dans chacune des phrases suivantes :

I . . . . live . . . . in Los Angeles before the earthquake.

I . . . . have . . . . a friend there who then . . . . move . . . . to New York. The day of the earthquake, we . . . . be . . . . in the supermarket where we . . . . shop . . . . every day. It was terrifying because everything . . . . fall . . . . from the shelves. But we . . . . survive . . . . !

7 Écris un petit texte pour raconter ce que tu avais l'habitude de faire quand tu étais encore en maternelle et/ou en primaire, et que tu ne fais plus du tout maintenant que tu es en 3e.

Pronunciation

Prononcer la terminaison *-ing*

1 a. Écoute les mots ci-dessous en faisant bien attention à la prononciation de la terminaison *-ing* :
track 24

*evening – destr**oy**ing – **batt**ling – **try**ing – heart-**brea**king – **floo**ding*

b. Entraîne-toi à prononcer ces mots.

c. Maintenant écoute et répète ces phrases. track 25

1. Good even**ing**, ladies and gentlemen.

2. First, the latest on the terrible wildfire that is destroy**ing** California.

3. Firefighters are battl**ing** day and night try**ing** to contain it.

4. An official has described the scene as "heart-break**ing**".

5. Significant flood**ing** has already been reported.

d. Quelle conclusion en tires-tu ?

La terminaison *-ing* se prononce-t-elle comme dans les mots français empruntés à l'anglais (*camping* par exemple) ? ☐ oui ☐ non

La syllabe *-ing* se prononce /. . . . . . . /, on n'entend pas le . . . .

5 Kia ora!

Discover

A whole world in one country

→ Textbook p. 60

3 a. Which extreme sports did you see?

- [ ] *Bungy jumping*
- [ ] *Canyon swinging and aerial obstacle courses*
- [ ] *Gliding and paragliding*
- [ ] *Climbing and abseiling*
- [ ] *Jet boating and jet skiing*
- [ ] *Kart racing*
- [ ] *Skiing and snowboarding*
- [ ] *Skydiving*
- [ ] *Skyjumping*
- [ ] *Zorbing*

b. Did you also see relaxing activities?

- [ ] *Swimming*
- [ ] *Kayaking*
- [ ] *Shopping*
- [ ] *Fishing*
- [ ] *Playing golf*

c. Now, explain why New Zealand is famous for extreme sports.

....

....

....

Key facts about New Zealand

→ Textbook p. 61

1 a. Let's find out what "quirky" means. Circle the adjectives you understand.

Thesaurus.com

quirky

quirky

Relevance + –

Common Informal

Synonyms for quirky

adj **eccentric**

bizarre
idiosyncratic
odd
off-the-wall
peculiar
strange
unconventional
unusual
wacky
weird
far out
freakish
freaky
in left field
kinky
out of the ordinary
outré
unorthodox
way-out

Antonyms for quirky

common
familiar
normal
regular
standard
usual
conventional

b. Now read the infographic. Can you solve these riddles? Underline the expressions in the infographic that helped you find the answers.

There are none in New Zealand, which makes you feel safe when you walk in the forest!

1. ....

There are so many of them each year that students learn some emergency procedures at school.

2. ....

You'll find some unique species of this animal in New Zealand, some of them even fly from Australia.

3. ....

You will have to learn it if you decide to become a New Zealand citizen one day...

4. ....

It is full of vitamins... but it is also the way people call themselves in New Zealand!

5. ....

One third of the country is covered in them.

6. ....

Environmentalists are happy that there is none in the country.

7. ....

A great number of them are made in New Zealand because the scenery is so spectacular!

8. ....

c. Select the quirkiest fact and explain your choice, using words from the list on p. 73.

....

....

....

....

....

Understand

A sacred ritual

→ Textbook p. 62

2 a. This article was published in the *Rotorua Daily Post*. Look at the map in your textbook p. 60. What is Rotorua famous for?

. . . .

b. Now read the editor-in-chief's opinion about *moko*:

Underline in red how the author feels about his moko.

Underline in blue the definition of moko given by the author.

ROTORUA Daily Post

Search keywords...

…ws | Opinion | Sport | Business | Rural | Life & Leisure

Moko more than tattoo

By Greg Taipari

7:00 PM Thursday May 30, 2003 — 13 comments

Moko is a visual representation of a person's genealogical links, personal achievements and connections to people and places of the heart. Moko for many Maori is a rite of passage, something which is earned or passed down from generation to generation. I have a moko and it is not a tattoo. I'm proud of it, it graces my body and it represents my whakapapa (genealogy). I don't see my moko as a bit of ink placed on my body, as a decoration or a fashion statement. It tells the story of who I am, where I've come from and, with my children represented in my moko, where my future lies.

Meet a Maori tattoo artist

→ Textbook p. 62

1 a. Watch the video, then write a caption under each picture.

Where?

....

Who?

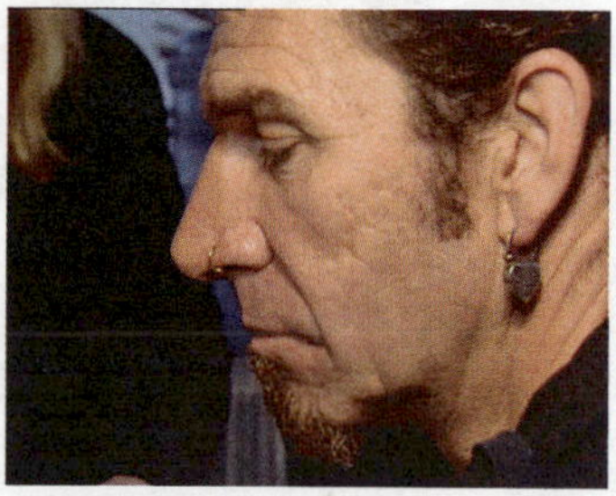

....

What and why?

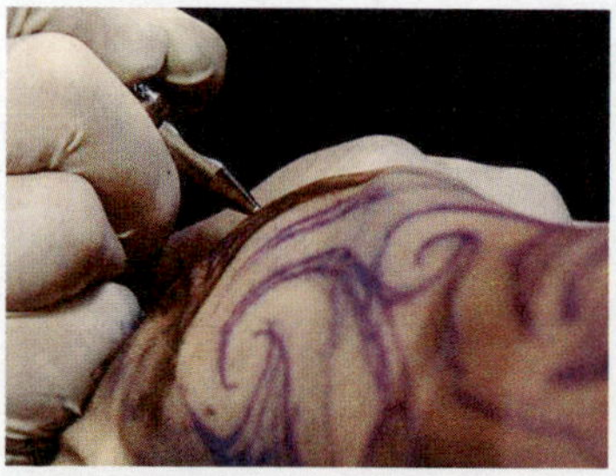

....

b. Watch the video again and check your captions. Complete or correct them when necessary.

Moko controversy

→ Textbook p. 63

3 **Read the title.** Then choose three different colours and underline in the text the elements that correspond to:

concern | ignorant use | Maori *moko*

tip
Attention, *concern* est un faux ami !

The New Zealand Herald

Concern over ignorant use of moko

3:10 PM Thursday Feb 27, 2003

A group of academics are concerned the Maori tattoo is being used by non-Maori, without understanding what the symbols mean.

Auckland University art history lecturer Ngarino Ellis and fellow academics Professor Ngahuia Te Awekotuku and Linda Waimarie Nikora were particularly concerned that people were "misappropriating" moko or traditional Maori tattoo.

The concern comes after controversy over heavy weight boxer and convicted rapist Mike Tyso's moko-looking tattoo over his eye, which he had done just before his fight against Clifford Etienne last weekend.

A spokesman for Tyson said it was meant to represent his being a "warrior".

Maori expert on facial tattoos Pita Sharples said at the time that he did not like seeing the design on Tyson because of his criminal past.

He was also disturbed by British rock star Robbie Williams' arm tattoo "because there are definitely Maori characters of moko" in it.

Ms Ellis said the fact that high profile figures like Tyson and Williams and musician Ben Harper were sporting moko-like tattoos, "demonstrates a need for more information in the wider community about moko, both here and overseas".

Training Task

→ Textbook p. 63

Is everyone entitled to have a Maori tattoo?

Think about:

Your role

....

Your point of view

....

....

....

....

....

....

Your feelings

....

....

....

....

....

....

Your arguments

....

....

....

....

....

....

tip

Tu vas intervenir à l'oral : ne rédige pas de phrases complètes.
Entraîne-toi à parler à partir de mots-clés.

Final tasks

Should France have been penalized? Debate.

→ Textbook p. 64

"France have been fined..." What is the meaning of "fine" in this context?

Fine

❶ *adj.* /faɪn/ **fin·er, fin·est**

1. Of superior quality, skill, or appearance: *a fine day; a fine writer.*
2. Very small in size, weight, or thickness: *fine type; fine paper.*

❷ *n.* /faɪn/

A sum of money required to be paid as a penalty for an offense.

v (tr) /faɪn/

To impose a fine on.

❸ *n. Music* /ˈfiːneɪ/

The end.

thefreedictionary.com

Words

❶ *Words to remember* Vérifie que tu connais le vocabulaire du chapitre.

→ Textbook p. 65

TRAVELLING ABROAD

Places

①  → .... → ....

②  paysage =  ....

③  = ...

④ .... ↖ ↗ ....

.... ← **This place is...** → ....

↓

....

Attitude

⑤ respect *(v)* ≠ .... ⑥ respect *(n)* → .... *(adj)*

⑦ offend *(v)* → .... *(adj)* ⑧ curious *(adj)* → .... *(n)*

People

⑨  *habitant* =  ....

⑩ .... a group of people living in the same area ....

⑪ tribal *(adj)* → .... *(n)*

Tourism

⑫ travel = → ....
→ ....
→ ....

Traditions

⑬ .... done as part of a ceremony ....

⑭  = ... ⑮ religious = ...

2 **Tu as reçu cette carte postale de Nouvelle-Zélande… pas en très bon état !**

Peux-tu tout de même la lire ?

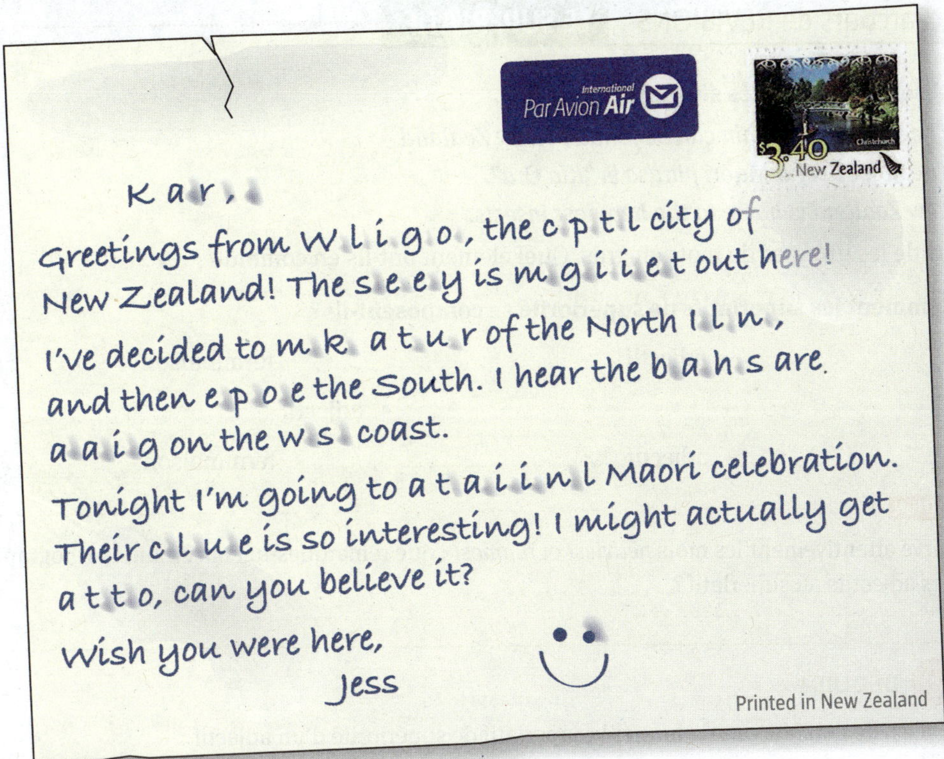

3 **Complète les phrases suivantes avec les termes appropriés.**

. . . . is an important industry in New Zealand. Last year 2.5 million visitors

. . . . the country.

New Zealand enjoys varied . . . . from cascading glaciers to active volcanoes.

The country needs to protect its Maori . . . . , including customs and traditions,

for future . . . .

Grammar

Parcours de RÉVISIONS : LE SUPERLATIF

a. Observe les énoncés suivants :

A. ***The smallest*** *dolphin can be found in New Zealand.*

B. ***The most useful*** *Maori phrase is "Kia Ora".*

C. *New Zealand is home to* ***the heaviest*** *insects.*

Regarde les groupes de mots en gras. Quel élément ont-ils en commun ? . . . .

b. Comment les superlatifs de supériorité se composent-ils ?

A. . . . . + adjectif . . . . + terminaison - . . . .

B. . . . . + ... + adjectif . . . .

C. . . . . + adjectif . . . . + terminaison - . . . .

ATTENTION

Observe attentivement les mots *heaviest* et *funniest* : que remarques-tu concernant l'orthographe de ces adjectifs au superlatif ? . . . .

DÉDUIS !

- Il existe deux façons de former le superlatif de supériorité d'un adjectif :

  1. *the* + adjectif + terminaison - . . . .

  Dans cette catégorie, on trouve les **adjectifs d'une seule syllabe** : *small, old, rare,* etc.

  2. *the* + ... + adjectif

  Dans cette catégorie, on trouve les **adjectifs de trois syllabes ou plus** : *unusual, peculiar,* etc.

- Pour beaucoup d'**adjectifs de deux syllabes,** le superlatif se construit selon les deux formes. Par exemple : *the heaviest insect ou the most heavy insect – the funniest sheep ou the most funny sheep.*
- Certains adjectifs de deux syllabes ne fonctionnent qu'avec *the most* : il s'agit entre autres de ceux terminés par *-ing (boring), -ous (jealous), -ful (useful), -al (fatal), -less (helpless), -ed (worried) et -ite (polite).*

ATTENTION

Mémorise ces deux exceptions : *good → the best* *bad → the worst*

Le superlatif d'infériorité est bien plus simple à construire. Quel que soit l'adjectif, on dira toujours : *the least* + adjectif. e.g. *This is the least expensive phone we have, sir.*

1 Parle des lieux suivants en utilisant le superlatif de supériorité :

e.g. Auckland – dynamic – place → Auckland is the most dynamic place in New Zealand.

1. Wellington – rainy – city

→ ....

2. Queenstown – beautiful – spot

→ ....

3. Franz Josef – impressive – glacier

→ ....

4. Rotorua – interesting – town

→ ....

5. The Bay of Islands – pretty – area

→ ....

2 Complète les phrases suivantes avec des superlatifs :

1. *The Lord of the Rings* is .... popular .... film shot in New Zealand.

2. The All Blacks are .... good .... rugby team in the world.

3. *Moko* is one of .... old .... traditions of Maori people.

4. The kiwi is .... famous .... bird in the country.

5. The pohutukawa tree is .... outstanding .... plant of the New Zealand flora.

1. LES QUANTIFIEURS

Many ou much ?

a. Lis les phrases suivantes :

A. ***Many** films were shot in New Zealand.*

B. *Celebrities like Rihanna or Mike Tyson don't show **much** concern about the moko.*

Dans ces phrases, comment se traduisent *many* et *much* ? ....

b. Regarde les mots *films* et *concern* :

Quelle est la différence entre les deux ? Films est au .... tandis que *concern* est au .... et ne peut pas se mettre au pluriel.

Ceci signifie que *film* est un nom ☐ dénombrable ☐ indénombrable et que *concern* est un nom ☐ dénombrable ☐ indénombrable.

DÉDUIS !

Many fonctionne avec les noms .... au ....
et *much* fonctionne avec les noms .... qui sont donc toujours au ....

(a) few ou (a) little ?

a. Observe les phrases suivantes :

A. *__Few__ Europeans would dare to have moko, it's too painful.*

B. *I have __a few__ friends who have moved to New Zealand; but it is a country that remains quite unknown to the French.*

C. *There's __little__ hope we can win the rugby match against the All Blacks, they are a lot stronger than us.*

D. *I need __a little__ help to convince my mom to let me have a tattoo.*

Europeans et *friends* sont des noms ☐ dénombrables ☐ indénombrables.
Hope et *help* sont des noms ☐ dénombrables ☐ indénombrables.
(A) little s'utilise donc devant des noms .... toujours au .... et *(a) few* devant des noms .... au ....

b. Traduis ces phrases dans ta tête. Que signifient :

- *few* et *little* ? ....
- *a few* et *a little* ? ....

DÉDUIS !

A few et *few* fonctionnent avec les noms .... au ....
et *a little* et *little* fonctionnent avec les noms .... qui sont donc toujours au ....

A few et *a little* permettent de dire ☐ un peu (il y en a, il y en a assez)
☐ peu (il n'y en a presque pas, pas assez).

few et *little* permettent de dire ☐ un peu (il y en a, il y en a assez)
☐ peu (il n'y en a presque pas, pas assez).

3 Quelle est la forme appropriée ?

1. Much / Many tourists rent a van to explore New Zealand.
2. Unfortunately, a few / few campsites are free.
3. Europeans know very few / little about the Pacific.
4. There are many / a few opportunities to discover Maori culture.
5. Much/Little of the area is mountainous, so you can do much / many hikes around here.

4 Imagine ta réaction à ces chiffres.

e.g. There are 3 million sheep in New Zealand → Really, that many?

1. This hat is 250 $. → Really, that .... ?
2. The Bay contains 144 islands. → Really, that .... ?
3. There are only 4.4 million inhabitants. → Really, that .... ?

2. *SHOULD HAVE / COULD HAVE / MUST HAVE* + PARTICIPE PASSÉ

a. Lis les énoncés suivants et complète les phrases :

A. *France*	*shouldn't*	*have*	*been*	*penalized for advancing on haka.*
B. *I think he*	*could*	*have*	*checked*	*with kaumatua (tribal elders).*
C. *That*	*must*	*have*	*hurt*	*the Maoris.*
	= ce sont des	= forme .... de *Have*	= verbes à la forme	

b. Ces structures permettent d'exprimer :

- une suggestion après coup : phrase ...... ;
- une hypothèse : phrase ...... ;
- un reproche / un jugement : phrase ....

DÉDUIS !

Pour exprimer un point de vue (suggestion, hypothèse, reproche...) à propos d'un fait passé, on a besoin d'un .... , comme *should, must, could* + l'auxiliaire .... à l'infinitif + le verbe à la forme ....

5 **Complète les phrases suivantes avec *could, should* ou *must* + *Have* + un verbe de ton choix au participe passé.**

1. The hall is so slippery! I was very lucky, I ....

2. I saw Esther crying this morning, I think she was looking for something: she ....

....

3. I can't lend you my jacket, I need it, you ....

4. I was so worried about you, ...

5. I can't see them anywhere, they you ....

6. She didn't even say goodbye, she ....

6 **Imagine la situation, puis complète les répliques suivantes. Compare tes réponses avec ton voisin et justifie tes choix.**

1. "I can't believe we lost this game! We .... win .... !"

2. "Did you say yes? You .... ask .... me first!"

3. "I'm so sad for her. She .... cry .... a lot."

4. "I don't know what I was thinking. I .... know .... better."

5. "They didn't have to go. They .... stay .... longer."

Pronunciation

Deux sons très particuliers de l'anglais : /ð/ et /θ/

1 **a. Écoute les mots suivants.** track 32

southern – enthusiast – other – both – wealth – thus – there – with – health – bath – bathe

Quel est le point commun à tous ces mots ? ....

ATTENTION à la prononciation de [th] ! De nombreux Français le prononcent soit /s/ soit /z/, alors que la prononciation correcte est /...../ ou /...../.

b. Classe les mots ci-dessus, selon la prononciation de [th] :

/ð/	/θ/

c. Trouve d'autres mots contenant /ð/ et /θ/ :

/ð/	/θ/

d. Quelle conclusion en tires-tu ?

La graphie [th] en anglais peut se prononcer soit /. . . . ./, soit /. . . . ./. Pour bien prononcer ces deux sons, il faut mettre la pointe de la langue entre les . . . . , sur la partie supérieure des incisives. Tous les mots contenant . . . . se prononcent ainsi, sauf de rares exceptions comme *Thames, Thyme, Thailand* et *Thomas* dont le [th] se prononce . . . .

2 Écoute ces phrases, et prononce-les en faisant bien attention au [th]. track 33

1. The landscapes in New Zealand are breathtaking.

2. Thanks to the wonderful weather, you can bathe in the Ocean almost every other day.

3. Theoretically, the weather is cooler in New Zealand than in Australia, but there can be some exceptions.

4. I think there are more sheep in New Zealand than New Zealanders. This can be considered as something weird for Europeans, but it's the truth.

6 Cool Britannia

Discover

Guess the British band!

→ Textbook p. 72

3 Homework – a bit of geography!

a. Locate the bands' hometowns or regions on this map.

b. Colour the map of the United Kingdom:

- Northern Ireland in green
- Scotland in blue
- England in red
- Wales in orange

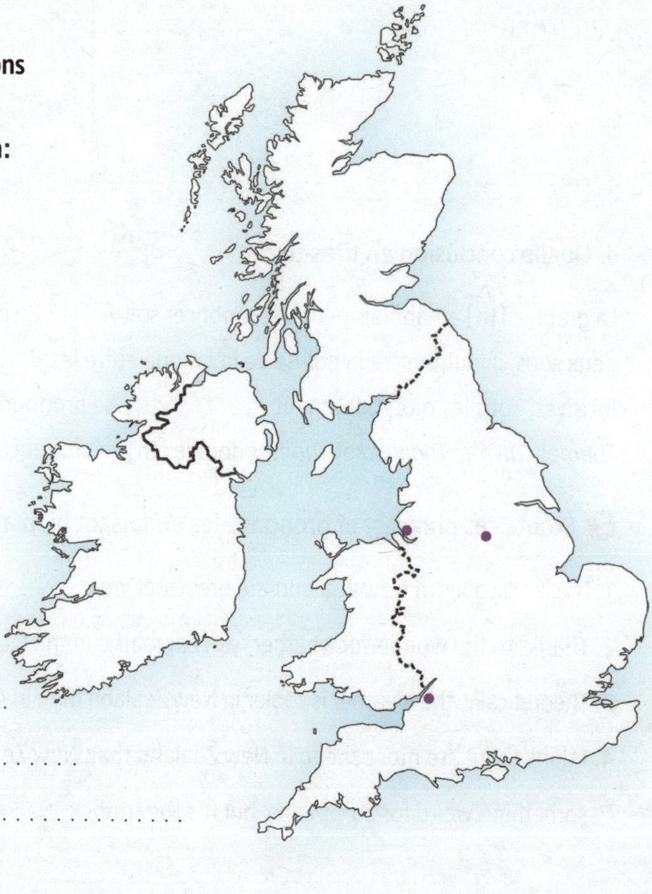

- Which country is not coloured in?

. . . .

- Why? . . . .

. . . .

. . . .

. . . .

. . . .

. . . .

c. Add five major towns to this map.

Also known as…

→ Textbook p. 73

2 Your turn! Before making up a new nickname, observe how the following ones are made.

The New Queen of Soul
The Godfather of Heavy Metal
The Prince of Darkness
The Pope of Mope

a. What do these nicknames have in common?

....

....

b. What do you notice about the pronunciation?

....

....

TOOLS

- a music genre
- a rhyme, rhyme *(v)*
- an image
- a superlative
- an alliteration (the repetition of a sound)

The Fab Four

c. What does "Fab" stand for?

....

What do you notice about the pronunciation?

....

....

The World's Greatest Rock and Roll Band

d. Identify each type of information and imagine a similar combination for another artist.

....

....

e. Now create your artist's nickname.

Tell it to the class. They will have to guess who your artist is.

Your band / singer →	Nickname
....	....
Your classmates' bands / singers →	**Nicknames**
....	....
....	....
....	....
....	....
....	....
....	....

Understand

"I've been hanging on the phone"

→ Textbook p. 74

4 Work on the rhythm and rhymes.

Miss You

I've been holding out so long
I've been sleeping all alone
Lord I miss you
I've been hanging on the phone
I've been sleeping all alone
I want to kiss you

Oooh

a. Count the number of feet for each line.

b. What effect does this pattern create?

c. Underline the stressed syllables in each line.

d. Now practise singing these lines!

Well, I've been haunted in my sleep
You've been starring in my dreams
Lord I miss you, child
I've been waiting in the hall
Been waiting on your call
When the phone rings
It's just some friends of mine that say,
"Hey, what's the matter, man?
We're gonna come around at twelve
With some Puerto Rican girls that are just dyin' to meet you
We're gonna bring a case of wine
Hey, let's go mess and fool around
You know, like we used to."

Aaah

Oh everybody waits so long
Oh baby why you wait so long
Won't you come home! Come home!

I've been walking Central Park
Singing after dark
People think I'm crazy
Stumbling on my feet
Shuffling through the street
Asking people, "What's the matter with you boy?"

Sometimes I want to say to myself
Sometimes I say

Oooh

I won't miss you child

I guess I'm lying to myself
It's just you and no one else
Lord I won't miss you child

Mick Jagger & Keith Richard, 1978

e. Find other rhyming pairs in the song.

Words

1 *Words to remember* **Vérifie que tu connais le vocabulaire du chapitre.** → Textbook p. 77

MUSIC

Artists

① . . . .

② . . . .

③ . . . .

④ . . . .

Performing

Donne un synonyme.

⑤ the public = ...

⑥ perform *(v)* = ...

⑦ 🇫🇷 *enregistrer un album* = 🇬🇧 . . . .

⑧ 🇫🇷 *être en tournée* = 🇬🇧 . . . .

⑨ 🇫🇷 *répéter* = 🇬🇧 . . . .

A song

⑩

parts of a song

. . . .

. . . .

. . . .

. . . .

. . . .

Donne un synonyme.

⑪ melody = ... ⑫ beat = ...

Instruments

⑬ .... ⑭ .... ⑮ ....

⑯ .... ⑰ .... ⑱ ....

⑲ ....

2 Choisis un groupe de musique que tu connais bien et décris le rôle de chaque membre du groupe.

....

....

....

....

....

3 Écris une petite critique.

- soit d'un concert ;
- soit d'une chanson que tu aimes (texte, mélodie, instruments, interprétation...).

tiP Tu peux t'inspirer de la critique du concert des Rolling Stones → Textbook p. 81.

....

....

....

....

Grammar

1. LES DÉTERMINANTS (1) : *THE* OU Ø ?

Les noms communs

a. Lis ce témoignage et concentre-toi sur les noms des genres musicaux :

- souligne ceux qui évoquent des genres en général ;
- entoure ceux qui sont définis précisément.

> "My favourite style is Ø metal, but only the modern genres like Ø progressive, and Ø avant-garde. I really don't like the metal music of the 1980s and early 1990s like Iron Maiden, Metallica, etc. But I also listen to Ø jazz and Ø funk from time to time."

b. Que remarques-tu quant à l'utilisation de l'article *the* ?

. . . .

c. Traduis ce texte en français.

. . . .

. . . .

. . . .

. . . .

d. Par quel(s) mot(s) as-tu traduit : *the* : . . . . ; Ø : . . . .

→ *The* et Ø peuvent donc tous les deux se traduire en français par . . . .

Les noms de pays

a. Lis ces noms de pays et complète le tableau :

Pays	Contient l'article *the*	Contient un nom commun	Nom du pays en français
France	☐ oui ☐ non	☐ non ☐ oui :	
The United Kingdom	☐ oui ☐ non	☐ non ☐ oui :	
The Netherlands	☐ oui ☐ non	☐ non ☐ oui :	

Great Britain	☐ oui ☐ non	☐ non ☐ oui :	
South Korea	☐ oui ☐ non	☐ non ☐ oui :	
New Zealand	☐ oui ☐ non	☐ non ☐ oui :	
The United States	☐ oui ☐ non	☐ non ☐ oui :	

b. Que remarques-tu ? . . . .

DÉDUIS !

Pour déterminer un nom, l'énonciateur utilise :

- l'article *the* pour évoquer ☐ quelque chose de précis ☐ quelque chose en général.
- l'article Ø pour évoquer ☐ quelque chose de précis ☐ quelque chose en général.

Devant les noms de pays, on emploie toujours . . . . , sauf dans quelques cas où l'on utilise l'article *the* lorsque le nom du pays contient un . . . .

En français, on utilise toujours l'article défini.

1 Complète l'article suivant à l'aide de *the* ou Ø :

Franz Ferdinand are giving their fans and listeners . . . . chance to choose their setlist[1] for . . . . BBC Radio 6 Music Festival.

Fans can select from a list of 15 singles, album tracks and B-sides. . . . . six songs that receive . . . . most votes will be . . . . opening six to be played by . . . . band.

Alex Kapranos, ... lead vocalist and . . . . guitarist of . . . . Franz Ferdinand, said: "We've never let . . . . fans choose . . . . setlist before. It wasn't my idea. Could be a total disaster. Could be amazing. Let's find out."

Sam Rigby, February 3rd, 2014, digitalspy.co.uk

1. setlist: *programme de chansons*

❷ Complète ces phrases à l'aide de superlatifs.

1. Pop is . . . . popular . . . . type of music in the UK.

2. Five of . . . . big . . . . . . -selling albums of 2012 were by British artists.

3. British artists have taken the gold and silver positions in . . . . . . good . . . . . . -selling albums of all time.

4. Queen's . . . . *Great* . . . . Hits is the first album to sell six million copies in the UK.

5. . . . . personal . . . . lyrics are often written by singer-songwriters.

6. And . . . . bad . . . . lyrics are those we used to sing when we watched cartoons!

2. *HAVE BEEN + V -ING*

a. Lis cet extrait de la chanson *Miss You*, et note la composition de la forme verbale en bleu :

I've been stumbling[1] on my feet
Shuffling[2] through the street
People ask me, "What's the matter with you boy?"

1. stumble: *trébucher*
2. shuffle: *marcher en traînant des pieds*

Sujet + auxiliaire . . . . au Présent + ... + verbe en . . . .

→ Ceci signifie que le verbe est conjugué au . . . . et que l'énonciateur a choisi d'y ajouter à la fois la forme . . . . + ... et la forme . . . . + ...

Cette forme sert à . . . .

Cette forme sert à . . . .

b. Relis la ligne verte : quelle est la conjugaison du verbe ? ☐ Présent ☐ Prétérit

→ Ceci signifie que l'ensemble se déroule dans le . . . .

c. Quel est le lien de sens entre les deux premières lignes et la dernière ?

Les deux premières lignes (c'est-à-dire les déambulations du narrateur dans les rues) permettent d' . . . . la réaction des gens à la troisième ligne.

DÉDUIS !

La forme *Have* au Présent + *been* + V *-ing* permet d'évoquer des actions qui ont déjà eu lieu (forme . . . . + ...) mais qui permettent de comprendre une situation (forme . . . . + ...), de l'expliciter au moment de parole.

3 Ces phrases sont toutes extraites du même conte pour enfants. Les personnages retournent chez eux et découvrent que les choses ne sont pas comme ils les avaient laissées.

a. Complète les phrases en choisissant les verbes et la conjugaison qui conviennent.

1. "Someone .... my porridge," growled the Papa bear.

2. "Someone .... in my chair," said the Mama bear.

3. "Someone .... in my bed and she's still there!" exclaimed Baby bear.

De quel conte s'agit-il ? ....

b. Imagine la réaction de *Teenage bear*.

....

4 Complète à l'aide des verbes entre parenthèses en choisissant la bonne conjugaison.

1. Adele is such a great singer! She .... sing .... since she was 5.

And shed .... record .... more than four albums.

2. – "You must know this band. Eric and Carmend .... perform .... together as The Blues Brothers in over 9.500 shows worldwide."

– "Id .... never/hear .... about them."

3. Emeli Sandé is exhausted. Shed .... rehearse .... for the last 2 weeks.

4. Unless youd .... live .... on a remote planet, you've probably heard this song!

Pronunciation

Les diphtongues /aɪ/, /eɪ/ **et** /ɔɪ/

1 a. Écoute les mots suivants, en prêtant attention aux lettres soulignées. **track 41**

noise – brain – time – pirate – wait – boy – child – choice – crazy – nickname – mine – wine – voice – play

Prononce-t-on les lettres soulignées avec un seul son voyelle ? ....

b. Ces sons sont appelés diphtongues, car ils contiennent .... sons voyelles, qui sont prononcés presque ensemble pour ne faire quasiment plus qu'un seul son.

c. **Classe les mots p. 97 dans le tableau, selon la prononciation de la partie soulignée ; puis ajoute d'autres mots contenant les mêmes sons :**

/aɪ/	/eɪ/	/ɔɪ/

❷ a. **Dans les phrases suivantes, souligne toutes les parties qui te semblent contenir les diphtongues /aɪ/ /eɪ/ et /ɔɪ/.**

1. This boy is being very noisy, it is time for him to stop crying.

2. I'm giving you the choice: either we watch Iron-Man or the Dark Knight. What do you think?

3. I've decided to take a plane to fly to Detroit for my boyfriend's birthday: I'm so excited!

4. Tom has been waiting for my sister outside because she forgot to write a note saying she would be out.

5. We really enjoyed the cake you baked yesterday; your pastries are a lot better than your wife's.

b. **Écoute ces phrases, et prononce-les en faisant bien attention aux diphtongues.** track 42

How to...

... write a draft *and not lose your mind!*

Entraîne-toi 2

Rappelle-toi : c'est un terme générique, vague.

❶ **Trouve un hyperonyme pour :**

1. violin .... **2.** classical music ....

3. singer..................................... **4.** whisper *(v)* ....

Rappelle-toi : c'est un terme précis, un exemple.

2 Trouve un hyponyme pour :

1. food ……………… **2.** wind instrument ………………

3. clothes ……………… **4.** people ………………

Entraîne-toi 3

3 Pense à des définitions en anglais pour désigner :

1. l'action de chanter faux ………………

2. l'Écosse ………………

3. un auteur compositeur ………………

4 Lis tes définitions à ton voisin pour tester leur efficacité !

Teste-toi !

5 Utilise le diagramme pour penser à des idées sur le sujet proposé et les organiser :

Examples: ………………

Counterexamples: ………………

Idea1 : ………………

Topic: **Should music be free?**

Idea2 : ………………

Examples: ………………

Counterexamples: ………………

7 The youngest state

Discover

First timers in Hawaii

→ Textbook p. 84-85

2 In groups. Work on one of these texts.

Mark Twain *In 1866, American writer Mark Twain went to Hawaii as a journalist for the* Sacramento Union. *He wrote letters to tell about his discoveries and experiences.*

Cap. Fitch said "There's the king. That's him in the buggy. I know him as far as I can see him."

I had never seen a king, and I naturally took out a note-book and put him down: "Tall, slender[1], dark, full-bearded; green frock-coat[2], with lapels[3] and collar bordered with gold band an inch wide; plug hat[4], broad gold band around it; royal costume looks too much like livery[5]; this man is not as fleshy[6] as I thought he was."

I had just got these notes when Cap. Fitch discovered that he'd got hold of the wrong king, or rather, that he'd got hold of the king's driver, or a carriage driver of one of the nobility. The king wasn't present at all. It was a great disappointment to me. I heard afterwards that the comfortable, easy-going king, Kamehameha V, had been seen sitting on a barrel on the wharf, the day before, fishing. But there was no consolation in that. That did not restore me my lost king.

The Letters Of Mark Twain, Volume 1, 1853-1866, by Mark Twain

1. *mince* – **2.** *redingote* – **3.** *revers* – **4.** *haut-de-forme* – **5.** *livrée* – **6.** *corpulent*

a. Who is "him"?

. . . .

b. Why? How do you think he must have felt?

. . . .

. . . .

c. What happened? How did Mark Twain feel?

. . . .

. . . .

. . . .

. . . .

. . . .

d. Imagine you were there with Mark Twain. Try to sketch the king's portrait:

→ Sum up Mark Twain's expectations and the reality of his experience:

Expectations
Reality / experiences
Feelings

Agatha Christie *In 1922, British writer Agatha Christie travelled around the world with her husband and stopped in Hawaii. She wrote about it in her autobiography.*

a. Locate these islands on a map.

b. What do you think they had imagined?

"We had a lazy voyage, stopping at Fiji and other islands, and finally arrived at Honolulu. It was far more sophisticated than we had imagined with masses of hotels and roads and motor cars. We arrived in the early morning, got into our rooms at the hotel and, straight away, seeing out of the window the people surfing on the beach, we rushed down, hired our surf-boards, and plunged into the sea. We were, of course, complete innocents. It was a bad day for surfing – one of the days when only the experts go – but we, who had surfed in South Africa, thought we knew all about it..."

Agatha Christie, *An Autobiography* (1977)

c. Imagine what they thought, and what surfing in South Africa had probably been like.

d. **Imagine the rest of Agatha Christie's day: write the diary page of that day.**

e. **Draw a sketch of Honolulu as Agatha Christie saw it.**

→ Sum up Agatha Christie's expectations and the reality of her experience:

Expectations

Reality / experiences

Feelings

Rick Bass *In the 1990s, American writer Rick Bass went to Hawaii on holiday with his family. This is the opening of his narrative.*

I was afraid I wouldn't like Hawai'i. I had expected to be homesick for the good, crisp weather of Montana the whole time I was there. I imagined it seething with traffic, sun and glimmer. I imagined that the Islands would be overrun with game-show winners and lit up with the terrible smiles of newly-weds[1].

If I head into Hawai'i's high mountains, I thought, into its upland rainforests, into its tortured, barren, exquisitely beautiful lava fields, I could stay clear of the crowded beaches. I was determined not to view Hawai'i as "paradise", not to even use that word, that cliché. For a while, at first, I saw the Islands as beautiful floating prisons [...]. And while that's true, I soon found that there was no other word — it was a paradise.

Rick Bass, *"Paradise Rising"*, in *Travelers' Tales Guide: Hawai'i, True Stories of the Island Spirit*

1. *jeunes mariés*

a. **Check where it is on the map at the end of your book.**

. . . .

b. **Why did he think he would find these people?**

. . . .

. . . .

. . . .

c. **Look at the map on p. 86 of your textbook: why did he see the Islands this way?**

. . . .

. . . .

d. Imagine what he told his friends and family before going to Hawaii...

....

....

e. Draw a sketch of Hawaii as Rick Bass was afraid of seeing it.

→ Sum up Rick Bass's expectations and the reality of his experience:

Expectations
Reality / experiences
Feelings

Training Task

"I just came back from Honolulu": complete trip reviews.

Traveller n° 1

I have just returned from an incredible island vacation. I spent a week or so on Kauai – then a week on Molokai. I must say that Molokai was everything I had been dreaming of and more ✍. I had read so many reviews from people complaining about dirty rooms or rude locals. Those people make me laugh. Molokai is not for everyone – and hopefully it never will be! I met the most amazing, open locals who took me in like family ✍. I explored the island, ate great food, in short had the time of my life!

Traveller n° 2

I just came back last night from Honolulu. Now I know I'm not really a beach person, but I was so bored on this vacation. I'm a solo traveller. Honolulu is so very commercial ✍. And I just couldn't find enough to do ✍. And the weather was awful ✍. I did walk up to, through, and back down Diamondhead. Nice workout. Nice photos. Anyway, Honolulu is not for me. Need a busier vacation spot.

1. **Read each review and identify the traveller's opinion of Hawaii now: ☺ or ☹ ?**
2. **Underline all the elements that show their opinions.**
3. **Use your findings in 1 and 2 to guess why they feel this way. What had they expected?**

Traveller nº 1:

....

....

Traveller nº 2:

....

....

4. **Choose one of the ✍ from each text above. Develop the review starting from that point: write a few lines to give more information about the traveller's expectations.**

Traveller nº 1: ....

....

....

....

Traveller nº 2: ....

....

....

....

Understand

A US state in the middle of nowhere

→ Textbook p. 86

1 Try to complete the captions around the map (use the Internet if necessary or ask your teacher questions...).

2 Find more people who have links with Hawaii and write similar captions.
Submit them to your neighbour and complete his or hers!

tip
Pense aux mots que tu vas saisir dans le moteur de recherche pour trouver l'information.

Australian-American actress
. . . .
was born in Honolulu.

American singer
. . . .
was born in Honolulu. Twenty years later, he came back and gave a concert there.

British writer
. . . .
surfed in Waikiki Beach.

This is the island where American writer
. . . .
spent 4 months as a journalist.

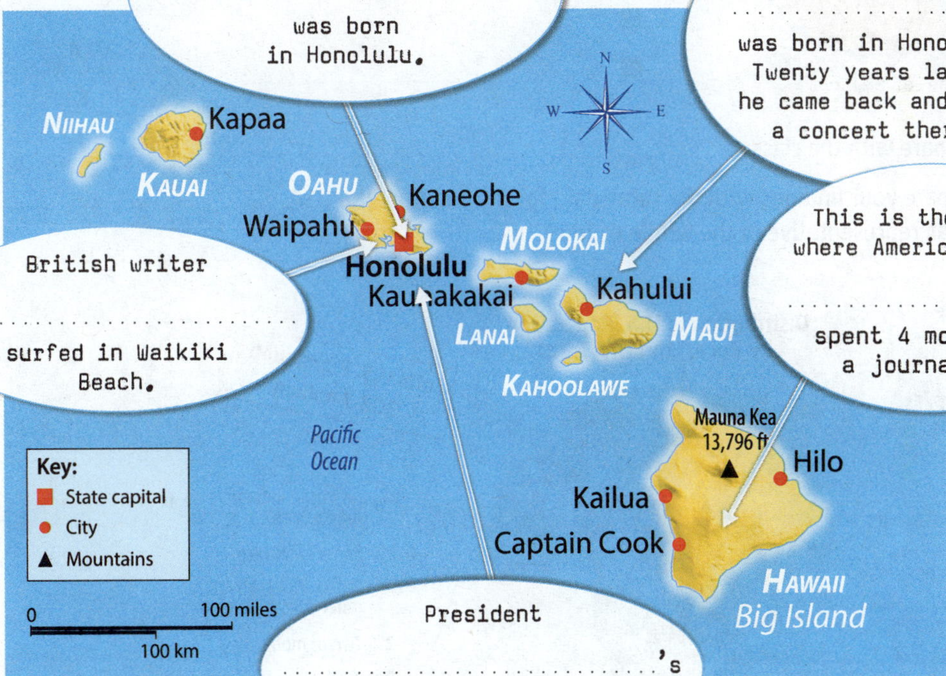

President
. . . .'s
favorite shave ice shop is here!

. . . .

. . . .

A multi-ethnic state

→ Textbook p. 87

6 a. In groups. Use everything you have discovered about Hawaii in this chapter to try to place the ethnic groups correctly.

Black – Two or more races – White – Native Hawaiian and other Pacific Islander – American Indian and Alaska Native – Hispanic/Latino – Asian

Ethnicity in Hawaii, July 2010

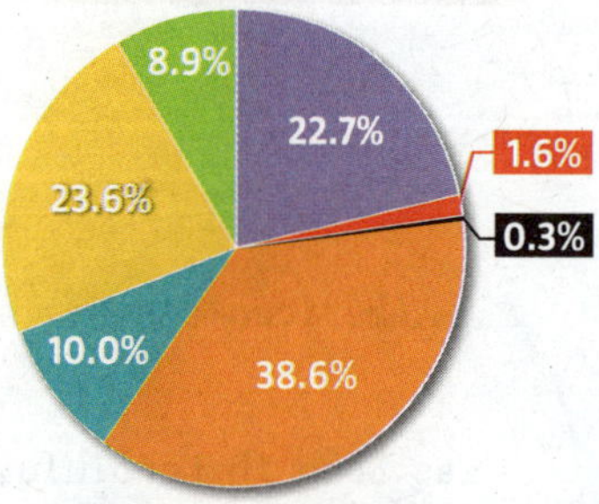

Key:

- ■ ....
- ■ ....
- ■ ....
- ■ ....
- ■ ....
- ■ ....
- ■ ....

b. Compare with the class.

c. Compare your findings with the same data for the whole of the USA. Is Hawaii representative of the whole country?

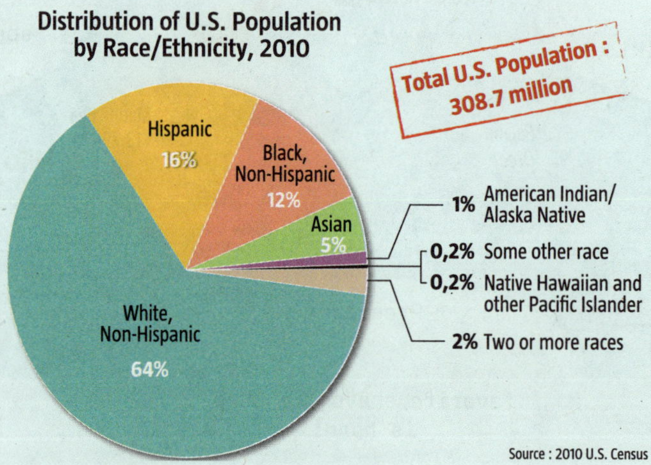

Words

1 *Words to remember* Vérifie que tu connais le vocabulaire du chapitre.
→ Textbook p. 89

TRAVELLING ABROAD (2)

People

① ethnically diverse = ...

② mainlander ≠ . . . .

③ tourist = ...

Travel

④ go ≠ . . . .

⑤ leave ≠ . . . .

⑥ travel by
- plane = ...
- boat = ...

⑦ . . . .

⑧ see the sights = do some . . . .

Impressions

⑨ 🇫🇷 *au début* = 🇬🇧 . . . .

⑩ 🇫🇷 *finalement* = 🇬🇧 . . . .

⑪ 🇫🇷 *« j'avais le mal du pays »* = 🇬🇧 . . . .

⑫ . . . .

⑬ . . . .

⑭ . . . .

⑮ . . . .

2 **Trouve dans ce chapitre des mots ou expressions pour parler de :**

....		....
....	**Hawaiian landscape / population**	....
....		....

....		....
....	**Experience and activities**	....
	....	

3 **As-tu bonne mémoire ? Voici des extraits de textes que tu as étudiés. Complète-les en te servant des indices fournis.**

"We had a .... adjective .... voyage, stopping at Fiji and other ...., and finally arrived at Honolulu. It was far more s _ _ _ _ _ _ _ _ _ _ ed than we had i _ _ _ _ _ ed with masses of .... places to stay .... and roads and motor cars."

"I was .... = "scared" .... I wouldn't like Hawai'i. I had .... = anticipated .... to be .... for the good, crisp weather of Montana the whole time I was there."

"I was d _ _ _ _ _ _ _ _ _ not to view Hawai'i as ".......... = heaven ....", not to even use that word, that cliché."

Grammar

1. *HAVE* AU PRÉTÉRIT + PARTICIPE PASSÉ

a. Lis les énoncés suivants :

A. *We [...] finally arrived at Honolulu. It was far more sophisticated than we had imagined.*

B. *We had surfed in South Africa and we thought we knew all about it.*

Quelle est la construction des verbes en rouge?

.... au Prétérit + verbe à la forme ....

Pour une fois dans ces phrases, l'anglais et le français se construisent de la même façon !

Comment traduirais-tu en français chaque verbe en rouge ?

La ville était bien plus sophistiquée que ce que nous ....

Nous .... *en Afrique du Sud, alors nous pensions tout connaître.*

→ Dans les deux cas, les événements évoqués en rouge ont eu lieu ☐ avant ☐ après ceux évoqués en vert.

b. Replace les propositions de chaque phrase sous le schéma :

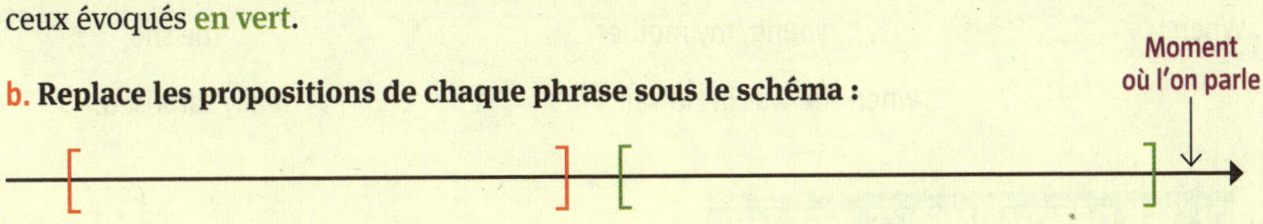

A. ....

B. ....

c. Mais ce n'est pas qu'une question de chronologie ! Relis bien chaque phrase : pourquoi l'énonciateur a-t-il recours aux formes en rouge ? Quel lien créé-t-il avec les parties en vert ?

....

DÉDUIS !

Have au Prétérit + participe passé permet :

- d'évoquer un événement qui est ☐ antérieur ☐ postérieur à un autre événement du ☐ présent ☐ passé ;
- de raconter ce qu'on pensait d'un événement, d'une action .... qu'ils ne se produisent.

1 **Conjugue le verbe, choisis entre *Have* au Prétérit + participe passé et Prétérit.**

Pour t'aider, classe les propositions dans l'ordre chronologique. Souligne ce qui s'est passé en premier en rouge et ce qui s'est passé ensuite en vert.

1. When my family .... (arrive) .... in Pearl Harbor, Obama .... (already/leave) .... the island.

2. Before Bruno Marse .... (become) .... famous, he .... (write) .... a lot of songs.

3. When I .... (see) .... a ukulele concert, I .... (be) .... amazed, I .... (never / hear) .... such beautiful sounds.

4. I .... (arrive) .... in my hotel in Honolulu and I .... (realize) .... that someone .... (steal) .... my keys.

5. When I .... (be) .... young, my mother .... (tell) .... me she .... (surf) .... when she was in Hawaii. I .... (be) .... really surprised.

2. LES DÉTERMINANTS *A* ET *THE*

A. *Here comes the king! That's him in the buggy.*

B. *I had never seen a king before.*

En **A**, l'énonciateur utilise *the* pour désigner le roi parce que, pour lui, ce roi est

☐ connu ☐ inconnu.

En **B**, l'énonciateur emploie *a* parce qu'il dit qu'il n'a jamais vu

☐ le roi d'Hawaii ☐ de roi en général.

DÉDUIS !

L'article qui permet de désigner un nom inconnu ou indéterminé, d'apporter une nouvelle information, est : ....

L'article qui permet de déterminer un nom, de le préciser, ou de parler d'un élément que l'on considère comme connu de l'interlocuteur, est : ....

2 Ajoute *a / an*, *Ø* et *the* dans les phrases suivantes :

1. .... last Queen of Hawaii left .... throne after .... coup d'état.

2. I saw .... documentary about .... Hawaii yesterday. .... documentary was very interesting. Especially .... part about .... manufacturing of .... surfboards.

3. I met .... great Hawaiian singer Israel Kamakawiwo'ole at .... end of .... concert. I learnt recently it was .... last concert of his life.

4. In Hawaii .... children don't spend much time watching .... TV. They prefer surfing or doing outdoor activities.

5. Hawaii is famous all over .... world for .... numerous pineapple plantations. But they also export .... other fruit and .... coffee.

Pronunciation

L'accentuation des mots en *-ity* et *-ety*

1 a. Écoute attentivement la prononciation et l'accentuation des mots suivants, puis répète-les. track 49

nobility – creativity – anxiety – activity – variety – society – simplicity – community

b. Indique où se situe l'accent primaire pour chacun d'eux.

c. Écoute les paires de mots suivants, et répète-les. track 50

noble – nobility	simple – simplicity	active – activity
creative – creativity	various – variety	electric – electricity

d. Sont-ils accentués sur la même syllabe ? ☐ Oui ☐ Non

Indique l'accent primaire pour chacun de ces mots.

e. Quelle conclusion en tires-tu ?

Lorsqu'un mot se termine par *-ity* ou *-ety*, l'accent primaire se place sur la syllabe qui ....

f. À ton tour, essaie de trouver d'autres noms se terminant en *-ity* ou *-ety*, et indique l'accent primaire pour chacun d'eux. Si le nom est dérivé d'un adjectif, écris cet adjectif, et indique également l'accent primaire (si tu ne le connais pas, cherche dans le dictionnaire).

How to...

... write a narrative *and impress your reader!*

Entraîne-toi 1

1 Relis le texte de Mark Twain et observe la manière dont l'auteur raconte l'anecdote.

Les premières paroles ne sont pas celles du narrateur. Ici, cela donne l'impression que le narrateur n'est pas maître de ce qu'il se passe.

Puis, le narrateur prend la parole, sans transition, afin de rendre plus fort le contraste entre les promesses du Capitaine et ses propres attentes.

Cap. Fitch said "There's the king. That's him in the buggy. I know him as far as I can see him."

I had never seen a king, and I naturally took out a note-book and put him down: "Tall, slender, dark, full-bearded; green frock-coat, with lapels and collar bordered with gold band an inch wide; plug hat, broad gold band around it; royal costume looks too much like livery; this man is not as fleshy as I thought he was."

I had just got these notes when Cap. Fitch discovered that he'd got hold of the wrong king, or rather, that he'd got hold of the king's driver, or a carriage driver of one of the nobility. The king wasn't present at all. It was a great disappointment to me. I heard afterwards that the comfortable, easy-going king, Kamehameha V, had been seen sitting on a barrel on the wharf, the day before, fishing. But there was no consolation in that. That did not restore me my lost king.

The Letters Of Mark Twain, Volume 1, 1853-1866, by Mark Twain

La description est longue et précise. Rien n'est laissé au hasard...

- Les éléments descriptifs sont organisés en fonction de leur longueur.
- Le narrateur donne déjà quelques indices quant à la chute... Repère-les.

Le narrateur annonce alors le quiproquo.

Observe comment il le fait :

- la structure de la phrase où il révèle le quiproquo ;
- les suppositions qu'il fait quant à la véritable identité de la personne qu'il vient d'observer (fais attention à l'ordre dans lequel il présente ces suppositions : quel est l'effet escompté ?).

Le narrateur fait part de sa déception, à trois reprises, de manière un peu exagérée : repère les mots qu'il choisit pour créer un effet comique (le décalage entre l'événement – bien peu grave en soi – et son ressenti).

Entraîne-toi 2

2 Voici un extrait de la nouvelle de science-fiction *The Fun They Had* (que tu peux retrouver dans son intégralité dans ton manuel p. 128).

Observe la manière dont le texte est présenté :

> Margie even wrote about it that night in her diary. On the page headed May 17, 2155, she wrote, "Today Tommy found a real book!"
>
> It was a very old book. [...]
>
> She said, "Where did you find it?"
>
> "In my house." He pointed without looking, because he was busy reading. "In the attic."
>
> "What's it about?"
>
> "School."
>
> Margie was scornful. "School? What's there to write about school? I hate school."
>
> *The Fun They Had*, Isaac Asimov (1951)

a. Entoure les guillemets : à quoi peuvent-ils servir ?

• ....

• ....

Les guillemets anglais remplacent donc les .... en français.

b. Regarde bien :

• **la ponctuation :**

– est-elle à l'intérieur ou à l'extérieur des guillemets ? ....

– quand on veut annoncer une citation après un verbe introducteur, en anglais on n'utilise pas les deux points (:), mais ....

• **la mise en page :**

– quand va-t-on à la ligne ? Chaque fois que ....

c. Relis la phrase : *She said, "Where did you find it?"*

On pourrait aussi dire : *'Where did you find it?'* she said.

Dans les deux cas, quel est l'ordre des mots en dehors des guillements : .... + ...

Comment traduirais-tu ces mots en français ? ....

Quelle différence remarques-tu ? ....

8 What if...?

Discover

Invisibility

→ Textbook p. 96

2 b. Listen to Michio Kaku's explanations and complete the diagram below:

- **with the necessary material**
  an object – microwaves / visible light – an invisibility cylinder [. . . . .]
- **with the verbs he uses to describe the actions**
  bend around – reform at the other end (. . . . .)

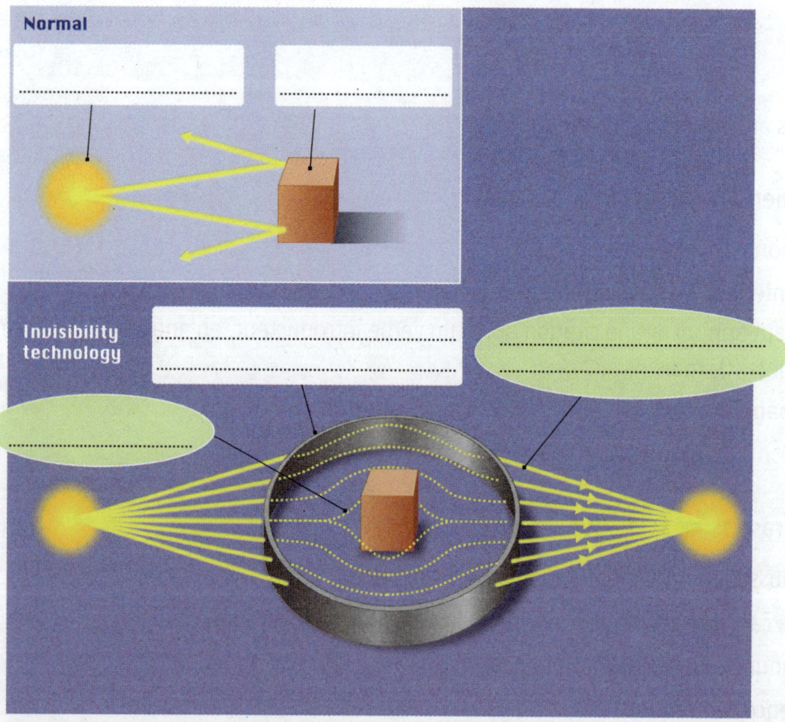

3 In groups. Get ready for your experiment.

	What Michio Kaku said	The objects you are going to use
The material you need	....	....

	What Michio Kaku said	How you are going to proceed
The different steps of the process	....	....

Outside the classroom

→ Textbook p. 96

Why not make your classmates guess what your parents told you?

What was supposed to be impossible when your parents were your age?	What could you say to make your classmates guess? Write down keywords you could use.	
....	Object / technology 1:	Object / technology 2:
How did your parents react when it became possible?	....	....
....		

After listening to your classmates, did anyone come up with the same examples as you?

☐ Yes! Which one? . . . .

☐ No. But I thought this one was funny: . . . . I should ask my parents about it!

Time travel

→ Textbook p. 97

"We all travel in time"

Is time travel possible?

Time travel is one of my favorite topics! I wrote some time travel stories in junior high school that used a machine of my own invention to travel backwards in time, and I have continued to study this fascinating concept as the years have gone by.

We all travel in time. During the last year, I've moved forward one year and so have you. Another way to say that is that we travel in time at the rate of 1 hour per hour. But the question is, can we travel in time faster or slower than "1 hour per hour"? Or can we actually travel backward in time, going back, say 2 hours per hour, or 10 or 100 years per hour?

It is mind-boggling[1] to think about time travel. What if you went back in time and prevented your father and mother from meeting? You would prevent yourself from ever having been born! But then if you hadn't been born, you could not have gone back in time to prevent them from meeting. [...]

http://spaceplace.nasa.gov/

Will it be possible soon?

I am confident time travel into the future is possible, but we would need to develop some very advanced technology to do it. We could travel 10,000 years into the future and age only 1 year during that journey. However, such a trip would consume an extraordinary amount of energy. Time travel to the past is more difficult. We do not understand the science as well.

An interview with NASA engineer
Dr Marc Rayman, 2013

1. intellectually amazing, astonishing

3 a. Read the first sentence of each paragraph. What do you learn?

. . . .

. . . .

b. In an article, the first sentence of each paragraph is like an introduction to what comes next.

- **Read the whole paragraphs and underline in each one the information that corresponds to the first sentence.**

  → Check with your classmates. Do you all agree?

c. Now use the elements you have underlined to recap what you have understood.

e.g. Dr Rayman thinks we all travel in time because...

Training Task

→ Textbook p. 97

Learn how to time travel!

1 a. Watch the video once and just enjoy the show!

b. Write down all the words you have understood. Underline those which seem important.

c. Watch the video again and identify:

The required material and conditions	
The different steps of the process	

2 Conclude.

- **Do Dr Hawking and Dr Rayman agree on time travel?**

....

....

- **Is time travel possible anytime soon?**

....

....

Understand

Three great myths, three great novels

→ Textbook p. 98

3 Work in groups.

Time travel

a. Identify the characters' dreams. Underline them in each text.

tiP

Puisqu'il s'agit de rêves, de choses hypothétiques, quels mots peux-tu rechercher dans les textes pour les repérer ?

b. Imagine other continuations to these sentences.

The Time Machine

The scientist has just told a group of guests about the time machine he has built. They are now discussing the advantages of such a machine.

"It would be remarkably convenient for the historian," the Psychologist suggested. "One might travel back and verify the accepted account[1] of the Battle of Hastings[2], for instance!" [...]

"Then there is the future," said the Very Young Man. "Just think! One might invest all one's money, leave it to accumulate at interest, and hurry on ahead!"

The Time Machine, H. G. Wells (1895)

1. *le récit communément admis* – **2.** battle fought in 1066 between England and France

"It would be remarkably convenient for" ....

....

....

"Then, there is the future. Just think! One might" ....

....

....

Invisibility

The Invisible Man

The Invisible Man is telling his friend Kemp about the night when he discovered how to become invisible.

"I remember that night. It was late at night [...]. It came suddenly, splendid and complete into my mind. I was alone; the laboratory was still, with the tall lights burning brightly and silently. In all my great moments I have been alone. 'One could make an animal – a tissue – transparent! One could make it invisible! All except the pigments. I could be invisible!' [...] To do such a thing would be to transcend magic. And I beheld[1], unclouded by doubt[2], a magnificent vision of all that invisibility might mean to a man,—the mystery, the power, the freedom."

The Invisible Man, H. G. Wells (1897)

1. saw – **2.** without douting

c. Imagine what these would be:

....

....

....

....

....

Eternal youth

d. Then what would happen? What would be the advantages?

. . . .

. . . .

. . . .

. . . .

. . . .

. . . .

. . . .

. . . .

The Picture of Dorian Gray

At the beginning of the novel, young Dorian Gray discovers a portrait that has been made of him.

"How sad it is!" murmured Dorian Gray with his eyes still fixed upon his own portrait. "How sad it is! I shall grow old, and horrible, and dreadful. But this picture will remain always young. It will never be older than this particular day of June... If it were only the other way! If it were I who was to be always young, and the picture that was to grow old! For that – or that – I would give everything! Yes, there is nothing in the whole world I would not give! I would give my soul for that!"

The Picture of Dorian Gray, Oscar Wilde (1890)

e. Share your ideas with the class.

Training Task

→ Textbook p. 99

"If you could have any superpower, what would it be?"

1 a. Listen and report what you have understood. track 52-53

Lianne's ideal power:

. . . .

. . . .

→ **Reasons**

. . . .

. . . .

. . . .

. . . .

. . . .

Olivers's ideal power:

. . . .

. . . .

→ Reasons →

. . . .

. . . .

. . . .

. . . .

. . . .

b. Listen again. Note down any expression that you think may be useful to explain your ideal power.

. . . .

. . . .

. . . .

2 Get ready to ask and answer questions about special powers.

Special powers	Questions	Answers
e.g. Invisibility	Would you like to be invisible? What would you do if you could be invisible?	Yes, I would love to be invisible! If I could be invisible, I would sneak out of class :-)

tip

Attention à la construction de tes questions : "What **would** you do if you could..."
aux. S BV

Words

❶ *Words to remember* **Vérifie que tu connais le vocabulaire du chapitre.** → Textbook p. 101

INVENTING THE FUTURE

Progress

① I succeed in = ...

② scientific discovery = ...

③ invent = ... an idea.

Advantages

④ . . . . ful = ... ful ⑤ practical = ...

Endless possibilities

⑥ Teleportation allows you to go . . . . ever you like.

⑦ Come . . . . ever you want. ⑧ Take . . . . ever you need.

Gadget

⑨ An object, machine, or piece of equipment that has been made for some special purpose

= a . . . .

Feelings

	It is...		*I feel...*		*It is...*		*I feel...*
⑩	exciting	→	. . . .	⑫	. . . .	→	. . . .
⑪	. . . .	→	thrilled	⑬	. . . .	→	. . . .

Special powers

⑭ visible ≠ . . . . ⑯ mortal ≠ . . . .

⑮ appear ≠ . . . .

2 Complète les phrases suivantes :

1. I had the wrong key, so I never . . . . open the door.

2. She insisted so much that she finally . . . . persuading me to go.

3. Arthur . . . . with a great idea the other day. He said "let's design a time machine."

4. Scientists say they have achieved a major . . . . in the struggle against cancer.

5. "Do you . . . . telekinesis?" "Of course I do! Look, I just made your pen fly without even touching it!"

3 Les super héros et leurs pouvoirs

a. Retrouve l'arme de chacun de ces héros et explique ce qu'elle leur permet de faire.

e.g. *Wonder Woman's lasso can make her enemies surrender.*

Iron-Man — Ghost Rider — Wonder Woman — Captain America — Thor

a powered armor — *a shield* — *a lasso* — *a hammer* — *an enchanted chain*

b. À ton tour : pense à un super héro et fais-le deviner à ton camarade en lui décrivant les pouvoirs que lui donnent ses armes.

Grammar

1. EXPRESSION DE LA PROBABILITÉ, DE L'HYPOTHÈSE

If... would, could et *might*

a. Lis les énoncés suivants :

A. *If I had an invisibility cylinder, no one could see me.*

B. *If you went back in time, you would prevent yourself from ever having been born.*

C. *"One might travel back and verify the accepted account of the Battle of Hastings, for instance!"*

- **Regarde les propositions subordonnées : quelle est la conjugaison des verbes en vert ?**
  ☐ Présent ☐ Prétérit

Toutefois, les propositions (en **A** et **B** du moins) commencent par ......

Cela signifie que les verbes renvoient à ☐ des faits passés qui se sont produits
☐ des faits hypothétiques ou irréels.

Il en va de même pour la phrase **C.**

- Il faut toujours qu'il y ait concordance des temps entre une subordonnée et une principale. Par conséquent, selon toi, quelle est la conjugaison des modaux en rouge dans les principales ? ☐ Présent ☐ Prétérit

Si les modaux sont ici conjugués au ...., quelle est leur forme infinitive ?

- *could :* ...., qui permet d'exprimer la ....
- *would :* ...., qui permet de renvoyer à ....
- *might :* ...., qui permet d'exprimer la ....

Toutes ces phrases renvoient donc à des situations .... mais en fonction du modal que l'énonciateur choisit d'employer, il pourra exprimer des nuances supplémentaires (possibilité avec le modal ...., grande incertitude avec le modal ....).

DÉDUIS !

- Pour exprimer des hypothèses, on peut utiliser des structures du type :

If + S + V au .... + compléments éventuels , S + ... + V à ....

proposition subordonnée — proposition principale

Dans la première partie de la phrase, le Prétérit permet d'évoquer :

☐ une situation dans le passé ☐ une situation irréelle, qui n'existe pas.

Dans la deuxième partie de la phrase, on imagine ce qui arriverait / pourrait arriver / risquerait d'arriver, etc. Relie les modaux à ce qu'ils expriment :

– *would* • • une hypothèse avec une notion de capacité.

– *could* • • une hypothèse que l'énonciateur considère comme possible un jour.

– *might* • • une hypothèse dont l'énonciateur doute beaucoup.

Dans l'exemple **c**, on remarque qu'il n'y a pas toujours besoin d'une subordonnée en *if* + verbe au Prétérit si la situation est ancrée dans l'irréel.

ATTENTION

Seul le verbe *Be* garde la trace du fait que ce Prétérit ne renvoie pas au passé, mais à un avenir hypothétique, comme on le voit dans l'extrait de *The Picture of Dorian Gray* où *Be* a une conjugaison particulière : *"If it were I who was to be always young, I would give everything!"* (l. 7 du texte p. 99 de ton manuel).

1 Complète les énoncés suivants en conjuguant les verbes en gris :

1. If you .... be .... a superhero, who .... you / be .... ?

2. That superpower .... change .... her life if she .... have .... it.

3. If human beings .... be .... invincible, some problems .... happen .... soon.

4. A lot of patients .... be saved .... if doctors .... find .... a cure against cancer.

5. If I .... build .... a time machine, I .... travel .... back in time, to Ancient Rome.

2 Imagine : *what might / could the world be like in the year 7510?*

....

....

....

....

2. *MAKE* + ADJ / + V

a. Lis les énoncés suivants et complète le tableau.

	Conjugaison du verbe *make*	Nature des mots en vert	Nature des mots en bleu
A. *Two weeks ago, scientists made a small object disappear.*		☐ Nom ☐ Prénom ☐ Verbe	☐ Verbe ☐ Adjectif
B. *The cylinder makes the object invisible.*		☐ Nom ☐ Prénom ☐ Verbe	☐ Verbe ☐ Adjectif
C. *Scientific improvements can make people immortal.*		☐ Nom ☐ Prénom ☐ Verbe	☐ Verbe ☐ Adjectif
D. *Michio Kaku makes me laugh.*		☐ Nom ☐ Prénom ☐ Verbe	☐ Verbe ☐ Adjectif

DÉDUIS !

Lorsque l'on souhaite parler de quelque chose ou de quelqu'un sur lequel on agit, on emploie, selon les besoins :

- sujet + ... (conjugué) + nom / pronom + ... (e.g. A, D).
- sujet + ... (conjugué) + nom / pronom + ... (e.g. B, C).

3 Comment dirais-tu en anglais ?

1. Un jour, la science nous rendra immortels.

. . . .

2. Mon super pouvoir pourrait me faire disparaître et réapparaître quand je veux.

. . . .

3. Le soleil était si fort qu'il a fait fondre les pneus.

. . . .

4. La kryptonite rend Superman faible et vulnérable.

. . . .

Pronunciation

Les *question-tags*

1 a. Observe les phrases suivantes, et plus particulièrement les parties soulignées :

1. You have a superpower, <u>don't you</u>?

2. Invisibility doesn't exist, <u>does it</u>?

3. She can become invisible, <u>can't she</u>?

4. Curing all diseases is a dream, <u>isn't it</u>?

5. It would be fantastic if you could have some sort of superpower, <u>wouldn't it</u>?

Comment appelle-t-on les parties soulignées ? À quoi servent-elles ?

. . . .

Que peux-tu dire de la forme des *question-tags* ?

Un *question-tag* se forme généralement en utilisant la forme inverse de l'énoncé devant lequel il se place. Si l'énoncé est à la forme affirmative (+), le *question-tag* sera à la forme . . . .
Si l'énoncé est à la forme négative (–), le *question-tag* sera à la forme . . . .

b. L'intonation des *question-tags* peut-être de deux sortes : montante ou descendante. Mais cela ne signifie pas la même chose. Écoute ces phrases avec une intonation différente pour chaque *question-tag*, et indique ce que cela signifie. track 57

1. You have a superpower, <u>don't you?</u> → . . . .

2. You have a superpower, <u>don't you?</u> → . . . .

3. She can become invisible, <u>can't she?</u> → . . . .

4. She can become invisible, <u>can't she?</u> → . . . .

5. Invisibility doesn't exist, <u>does it?</u> → . . . .

6. Invisibility doesn't exist, <u>does it?</u> → . . . .

c. Quelle conclusion en tires-tu ?

Lorsqu'un *question-tag* négatif dans une phrase affirmative ou un *question-tag* affirmatif dans une phrase négative a une intonation . . . ., il se rapproche d'une vraie question, et l'énonciateur demande réellement l'avis de son interlocuteur.

Lorsqu'un *question-tag* négatif dans une phrase affirmative ou un *question-tag* affirmatif dans une phrase négative a une intonation . . . ., il se rapproche d'une « fausse » question, et l'énonciateur ne demande pas réellement l'avis de son interlocuteur, mais juste une simple confirmation.

2 a. Observe maintenant ces *question-tags*. Que peux-tu en dire quant à la forme et à l'intonation ?

1. You could become invisible one day, could you?

2. You don't have any superpower, don't you?

3. She is invisible, is she?

4. He can cure diseases, can he?

b. Vérifie tes réponses en écoutant ces phrases. track 58

c. Quelle conclusion en tires-tu ?

Lorsqu'un *question-tag* conserve la même forme (affirmatif ou négatif) que dans l'énoncé, l'intonation est toujours .... L'énonciateur ne demande pas réellement l'avis de son interlocuteur, ni une simple confirmation, mais exprime sa surprise, et souvent une certaine ironie. Prépare des phrases contenant des *question-tags* en prenant bien soin de choisir soit une intonation descendante, soit une intonation montante, selon ce que tu veux dire. Lis ensuite ces phrases à un camarade, qui devra, ou non, répondre, selon l'intonation choisie.

....

....

....

How to...

...use a dictionary *and not Google traduction!*

Entraîne-toi 2

1 Identifie les abréviations ci-dessous, et fais correspondre les mots qui suivent :

n.	*adj.*	*v.*	*adv.*	*prep.*	*idiom.*
to	*scientist*	*kill*	*pretty*	*what's up ?*	*really*

2 Trouve la forme radicale (infinitif pour les verbes, singulier pour les noms) de chacun des mots en gras, puis cherche-les dans un dictionnaire (unilingue ou bilingue).

1. He was **lying** on the floor, unconscious, when I walked in. → ....

2. Look at these **geese**! They're enormous! → ....

3. When I grabbed the invisibility cloak, I **ripped** it apart. → . . . .

4. The scientist **conveyed** a feeling of enthusiasm and passion. → . . . .

Teste-toi !

1 Trouve la traduction des mots en gras :

1. Si j'avais **une baguette magique**, je changerais le monde. → . . . .

2. Achète-moi **une baguette de pain** ! → . . . .

3. J'adore Roméo et Juliette, c'est ma **pièce** préférée. → . . . .

4. Tu m'as donné une fausse **pièce** de 1 euro ! → . . . .

2 Trouve la traduction du mot en gras :

1. This is a special clock, it has no **hands**: it's a time machine ! → . . . .

2. Show me the palm of your **hand**, so I can tell your future. → . . . .

3 Les mots suivants ont plusieurs sens, essaie de les trouver, puis vérifie dans un dictionnaire.

Pour chaque mot, fais une phrase illustrant l'une de ses significations. Soumets tes phrases à ton voisin.

1. *date* . . . .

. . . .

2. *right* . . . .

. . . .

3. *rose* . . . .

. . . .

4. *type* . . . .

. . . .

9 Together for a year

Discover

"I got my yearbook today!"

→ Textbook p. 108

2 b. Note down Ashley's comments about each of these pages.

1

. . . .

. . . .

. . . .

2

3

4

5

. . . .

. . . .

3 a. Try to imagine the layout of the page Ashley is commenting on.

- What's the title of the page? Clue: what word does Ashley repeat many times?
- Note down the different categories.
- For each category, note down the names you hear.
- Note down the main title and categories.
- For each category, note down the information you understand.

Yearbook staff

→ Textbook p. 108-109

2 Need help? **a. Underline what you find most motivating about working on the yearbook:**

Reasons to Join Yearbook

- Honors Credit
- Practical Arts Credit
- Computer Competency Credit
- Looks good to colleges because it shows them:
  - ☑ You know how to meet a deadline and can work under pressure
  - ☑ You have leadership and organizational skills

What Students do in Yearbook

- Create a 400-page, all-color yearbook
- Write all copy, take all pictures, and create all pages in the yearbook
- Preserve student memories of a single year

Honors Special credit or recognition given to students who have successfully done work at a high level.
e.g. *She graduated with (top/high) honors.*

Credit A unit that measures a student's progress towards earning a degree in a school, college, etc.
e.g. *So far, you've earned a total of 12 credits.*

College (US) A school you go to after high school.

Explain why: ....

....

....

b. Associate each role (writer/photographer/page designer) with the necessary skills. Then justify your choices orally.

creative • responsible • hardworking • dedicated • good time managers

Writers

Interview students, write stories and write captions

Photographers

Attend sports games, club events and other events to take pictures

Page Designers

Lay out and design each of the 400 pages of the yearbook

c. Write more adjectives for each role.

tiP Use Thesaurus.com

....

....

....

....

d. Now which of these jobs would fit you best? Explain why.

....

....

....

....

....

....

Training Task

→ Textbook p. 109

Let's get started on the class yearbook!

1 Get ready for your presentation. Write down some words that will help you convince your friends that you are the right person for the role you have chosen. Think of your:

experience *skills* *interests* *personality* *motivations*

Role chosen: ....

....

....

....

....

2 Circle the words you will stress, and check their pronunciation on www.merriam-webster.com.

Understand

School events & Students' pages

→ Textbook p. 110 – 113

In groups. Choose one of the following sections and study it together.

1. Sports → Textbook p. 110

1 Look at the pictures. Can you identify each sport?

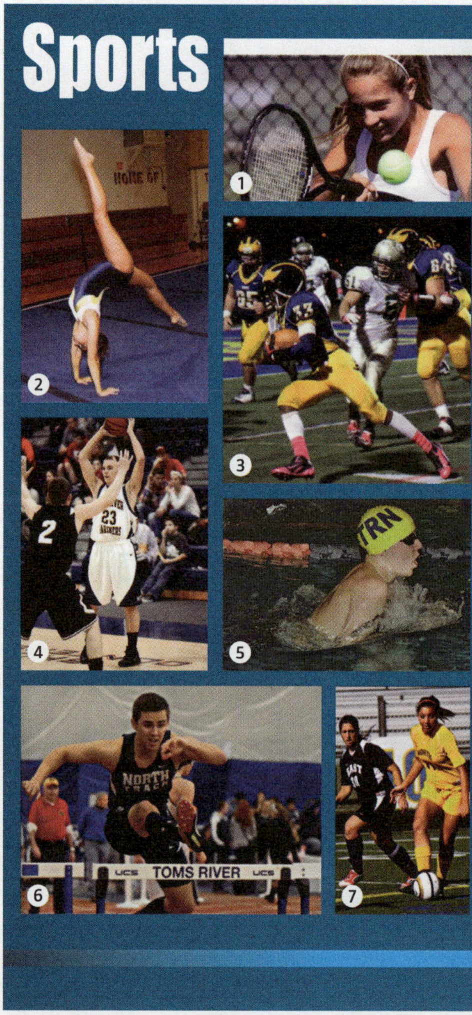

[Say what?]

"I love being part of a team and, honestly, the girls I've met and come to know are the best group of girls around."
Christy [redacted], senior

"I like X.C because I like running outdoors on natural terrain. The members are pretty awesome and it keeps me off my couch too. Triple win!"
Brandon [redacted], junior

"Track gives me something to do instead of just going home and sleeping, so I can stay in shape and make friends. Running is one of my only stress relievers."
Anthony [redacted], sophomore

"I like softball because I love my teammates and we get along like a family"
Jenna [redacted], freshman

① ....

② ....

③ ....

④ ....

⑤ ....

⑥ ....

⑦ ....

2 What do "X.C" and "Track" consist in? What is the difference between them?

....

....

....

3 Google this sport to learn what it is. Explain it.

....

....

....

4 What do these "Say What?" quotes have in common? Note down some key expressions:

. . . .

. . . .

. . . .

5 What about sports in your school? Do they play a similar role?

Discuss it with your group, and take notes for your presentation.

2. Junior prom → Textbook p. 111

"Down the Shore"

JUNIOR PROM

The Toms River North Junior Prom Committee did an outstanding job decorating the Poland Springs Arena for the "Down the Shore" theme. There was amazing food, boardwalk games and even sand! To the far right, Josh [illegible] and Tyler [illegible] stand at one of the many spots to take pictures at the beginning of the night. The photo booth was another hot spot of the evening. The blue and gold beach chairs were also a big hit when the students first entered the Pine Belt Arena. The wooden chairs gave the juniors an opportunity to sign their names so the Class of 2013 will never be forgotten. As the students entered the dance floor, they really seemed to be dancing on the beach. The food was catered by Famous Daves and everyone loved it! At the climax of the night, the prom king and queen were announced. The winners were Chris [illegible] and Maddie [illegible]. The students could not be happier with the results. As the night came to an end, the last song was played and all the juniors gathered together on the dance floor for the last dance. The Class of 2013 junior prom was a huge success and was most definitely a night to remember.

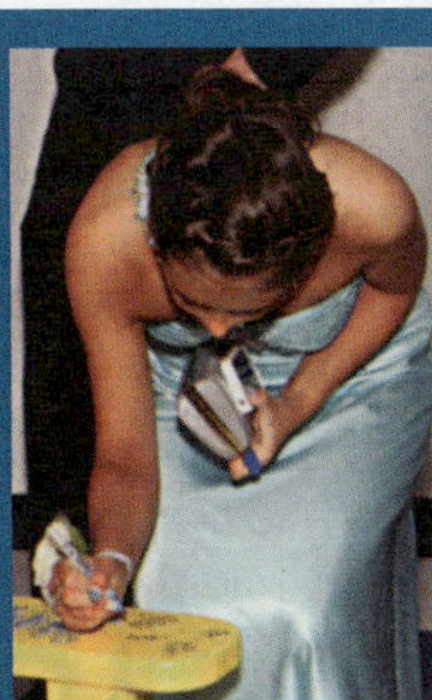

1 What is junior prom? Use the pictures to suggest a definition.

Junior prom is . . . .

. . . .

2 Read the text. Use different colours to underline the key words corresponding to:

Who *Where* *When* *Why*

3 Could this event be organized in your school? Discuss it with your group, and take notes for your presentation.

. . . .

. . . .

. . . .

3. Students' pages → Textbook p. 112

Charlotte Boundy

House: TL

Name: Charlotte Boundy

Nickname: Lady Majestic, The Bunny, Chez

Most likely to be: singing, dancing, eating

Most likely to say: "you'll never guess what happened!"

How do you sum up Charlotte? I remember her at the beginning of my Highgate life when I was sitting next to her in maths and she wrote on Tinkerbelle paper, I didn't imagine I would somehow end up being good friends with her a few months later… We were antitheses of each other, still are, but we've grown close and "acclimatised" to each other. Her joyful nature and incredibly lively character always make people smile. She is always kind and caring and will make you laugh when you're down, even if it is with a completely outrageous comment… QUIET is not an adjective Charlotte will ever be associated with. I assure you that you'll know when she is in the room.

There is rarely a day when she arrives in school without a story about something dramatic that's happened to her or a strange dream to share. The phrase "you'll never guess what happened to me" springs to mind and honestly, you would never guess. Her dedication and passion for performing arts and drama is evident, she pirouettes in any space big enough and she will get involved in every play possible, no matter how much she is already doing. One thing I will never do is get into a car with her, unless I was driving. I would prefer to stay alive… Overall, it's very hard to think of a single word to fit her so she is therefore, indescribable.

Emma [redacted]

Joshua Pullinger

House: Westgate

Name: Josh Pullinger

AKA: JP, Joshi P, Keith and Pully

Time at Highgate: 8 years

Sports/societies/activities: Cricket, Football/Getting in touch with my feminine side, getting a bit too touchy with friends

Most likely to say: "Soooooo"

Most likely to be: Anything except being a teacher and I mean anything

Josh is an interesting person to be around. One thing he is not is boring, as he is always ready to make the situation funny or surreal. He is flamboyant and at times side splittingly funny. He can always make life, however dark it seems, brighter. He finds the smallest things amusing and indeed delights in some to such an extent we have doubts as to his mental age. Josh often feels the need to show his love and affection for others and he is a very affectionate person.

In addition he is well known in the school for his habit of saying whatever comes to mind, at all times. We have come both to admire the random junk that he comes out with and not to worry as to what exactly he will say. He has on many occasions angered me to the point of violence but I have never not been amused at the same time. I have faith in the fact that he will find his niche in life and that he will no doubt be very good at whatever oddball job he excels at. But I for one must thank him for all he has done to keep me sane.

Paul [redacted]

1 Who do you think wrote the students' pages above?
Circle their names, and imagine who they are.

2 Now split your group in two: some of you will read about Charlotte, the others about Joshua.

a. Read the text on the right. What aspects of the student did you learn about?

- ☐ personality
- ☐ academic achievements
- ☐ favourite activities
- ☐ family
- ☐ things he or she is famous for

b. Compare your findings with the other group.

3 Now read the information on the left. Make sure everyone understands each category.

4 Recap. What do these pages consist of?
Discuss the contents with your group and take notes for your presentation.

. . . .

. . . .

4. Just say it! → Textbook p. 111 & 113

1 Look at these three documents. How are they structured?

Just say it!

Finish this sentence: "I could not live without..."

"I could not live without my family in my life."
Quintin [illegible]

If you could switch places with any celebrity, who would it be? Why?

"I would switch places with Mila Kunis because she's a really talented actress and it would be fun to play one of the roles she has done."
Zeel [illegible]

If you could be invisible, what would you do?"

"If I was invisible for a day, I would scare people because I think it would be funny"
Adeline [illegible]

. . . .

. . . .

. . . .

2 How would you answer each of these questions?

1. . . . .
2. . . . .
3. . . . .

3 a. Individually, make a list of similar questions that could appear in your yearbook:

. . . .

. . . .

b. Share your ideas with your group and select the best ones for your presentation.

. . . .

. . . .

. . . .

4 Get ready to explain what this section consists of.

5. In ten years → Textbook p. 113

In ten years . . .

"In ten years, I want to be living in New York City doing something with finance."
Mike

"I would really love to be married and starting a family in ten years. I also want to be living in California and doing something with photography."
Emma

"I see myself graduate from college with a PhD in Physics in ten years."
Jess

"In ten years, I picture myself starting a family and having a job as a first grade teacher."
Nicole

Senior Carlie reads a book in preparation for her future. In ten years she would like to graduate college with a degree in Psychology.

Joey predicts that in ten years he will be involved in the computer world. He said he hopes to study the subject in college and become a successful computer engineer.

1 What is this page about? Individually, imagine the question that was asked then compare with your group.

. . . . in ten years?

2 **Read the different paragraphs, and complete column 3.**

Carlie		• graduate college with a degree in Psychology.
Nicole		• .... • ....
Mike		• ....
Emma		• .... • ....
Joey		• .... • ....
Jess	sees himself	• ....

3 **Now read the paragraphs again and complete column 2.**

4 **Individually, write down what *you* would answer.**

....

....

5 **Recap with your group and get ready to explain to the class what this section consists of.**

Words

1 *Words to remember* Vérifie que tu connais le vocabulaire du chapitre.

→ Textbook p. 115

SCHOOL YEARS

Education

① A school day is divided into several . . . .

② *une matière (maths, espagnol...)* = ...

③ A–, B+, C = ...

Sports

④ A match = a . . . .

⑤ Someone who is in the same team as you = ...

⑥ . . . . something that reduces stress

Clubs

⑦ *adhérer à un club* = ...

⑧ *voyage scolaire* = ...

Students

⑨ Someone who is in your class = ...

⑩ Someone who is in your school = ...

⑪ The students who are in the same age group as you = ...

⑫ ☺ — Students can be — ☹

. . . .

. . . .

Friendship

⑬ get on very well = ... ≠ ⑯  . . . .

⑮ things that are remembered
. . . .

⑭ se rapprocher = ...

Projects

⑰ success *(n)* → . . . . *(adj)*

⑱ a diploma = ... ⑲  = ... *(v)*

2 Cette annonce ne s'affiche pas correctement sur le site de Belmont High School. Saurais-tu la déchiffrer ?

BELMONT HIGH SCHOOL DRAMA CLUB

Come and @&# wlkfhjql us!

NEW ¶§dsfà! !°$ ALWAYS WELCOME

If you are...

Rpkfgkfdgpk* motivated 564r4ezéaf==

... then you should be part of our 'O23+3RJOXMlkùqdkk!

When is it on?

Every Wednesday evening 6:00 – 8:00

How to t^dmsk,<dptn''?

Download an Mμ*lkl''dkfkjkjK on www.belmontdramaclub.com

and ++*5666FDSSDFzmm^¨¨ it to Room 12

Hope to see you there!

3 **Qu'ont dit les professeurs de Kate dans son bulletin ?**

Kate Hutchinson

Subject	Grade	Comments
History	A +	Has made amazing . . . . this year.
Math	A	Kate can work under . . . . and she always meets . . . . Well done!
Spanish	B +	A . . . . student: keep up the effort!
Economics	B +	Very . . . . in class, but a good student.
Art	A –	Highly motivated, and extremely . . . . : she always has new ideas!

Pronunciation

Les mots en *-ic, ics* et *-ical*

1 **a.** **Dans ce chapitre sur les Yearbooks, tu as utilisé des noms de matières, tels que *physics*, *mathematics*, *economics*, *informatics*, etc. ou utilisé des adjectifs comme *dramatic*, *terrific*, *fantastic* ou *chronological*, *autobiographical*, *geographical*. Écoute attentivement leur prononciation et leur accentuation de ces mots, puis répète-les.** track 60

1. *physics* **2.** *mathematics* **3.** *economics* **4.** *informatics* **5.** *dramatic* **6.** *terrific* **7.** *fantastic* **8.** *chronological* **9.** *autobiographical* **10.** *geographical*

b. **Indique ci-dessus où se situe l'accent primaire pour chacun de ces mots.**

c. **Écoute les paires de mots suivants, et répète-les.** track 61

drama – dramatic *geography – geographical* *history – historical*
fan – fanatic *real – realistic*

d. **Indique l'accent primaire pour chacun de ces mots. Sont-ils accentués sur la même syllabe ?**
☐ Oui ☐ Non

e. **Quelle conclusion en tires-tu ?**

Lorsqu'un mot se termine par *-ic, -ics* ou *-ical*, l'accent primaire se place . . . . la syllabe contenant ces sons.